D0368454

# Growing an Evangelistic Sunday School

*organize an "assimilation"*

*New members must identify 7 new friends after 6 months to become active.*

*Hemphill on S.S.; 69*

*5 Teaching/Learning Principles; p. 142-144*

*Assimilation; 158*

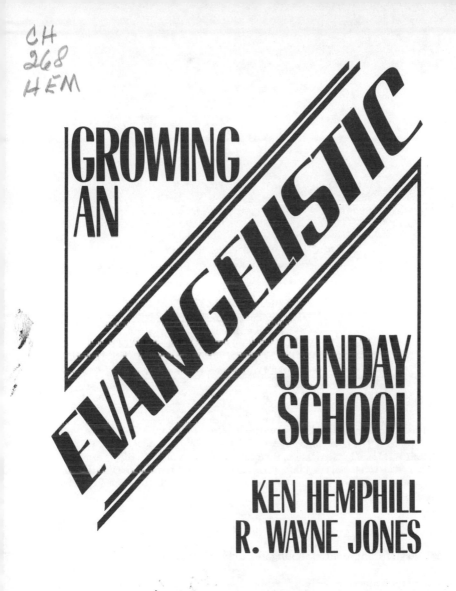

# GROWING AN EVANGELISTIC SUNDAY SCHOOL

## KEN HEMPHILL
## R. WAYNE JONES

**BROADMAN PRESS**
Nashville, Tennessee

ISBN: 0-8054-3243-4
Dewey Decimal Classification:
Subject Heading:
Library of Congress Catalog Card Number: 89-32313

Printed in the United States of America

Unless otherwise indicated, Scripture quotations are from the *New American Standard Bible.* © The Lockman Foundation, 1960, 1962, 1963, 1968, 1971, 1972, 1973, 1975, 1977. Used by permission. Scripture quotations marked (KJV) are from the King James Version of the Bible. Scripture quotations marked (NIV) are from the Holy Bible, *New International Version,* copyright © 1973, 1978, 1984 by International Bible Society.

**Library of Congress Cataloging-in-Publication Data**

Hemphill, Kenneth S., 1948-
   Growing an evangelistic Sunday School / Kenneth S. Hemphill, R. Wayne Jones.
      p.   cm.
   ISBN 0-8054-3243-4
   1. Sunday-schools. 2. Evangelistic work. 3. Sunday-schools-Growth. I. Jones, R. Wayne, 1953-   • II. Title.
BV1523.E9H4   1990                              89-32313
268—dc20                                        CIP

# Foreword

If you have been looking for *the one* book which combines Sunday School, evangelism, and church growth, look no further. This is it! *Growing An Evangelistic Sunday School* remarkably synthesizes the best classical and contemporary literature on Sunday School work, church growth, and evangelization. Especially does this volume address these three disciplines as they have been practiced historically by those Christians called Southern Baptists.

Ken Hemphill has discovered a striking similarity between basic Sunday School work and church growth methodology, particularly at the point of principles. He and Wayne Jones urge that the entire outreach program of the local church be merged with Sunday School ministry. Readers familiar with the writings of D. A. McGavran, Peter Wagner, Win Arn, and a host of others from the McGavran school of thought will probably resonate strongly with the ways in which this literature is so thoroughly integrated with the authors' thoughts on how to grow an evangelistic Sunday School.

Hemphill and Jones write out of their personal experience. They are not only familiar with the literature on their subject; they know what they are writing about from first-hand knowledge which they have learned through incarnational involvement in effective day-to-day ministry across the years. Their actual pastoral experiences in growing an outstanding evangelistic church through the Sunday School gives their book an authority and authenticity which appeals to the reader.

These authors believe that evangelism is the soul of the Sunday School. They are advocating Great Commission Sunday Schools. Nowhere do they make an arbitrary separation between the *kerugma* (preaching) and the *didache* (teaching) of the church. They advocate no clear-cut distinction between the work of the evangelist and the teacher.[1] I like that, because I too find no such hard-and-fast dichotomy between proclamation and teaching in the New Testament churches.

They do, however, see the pastor as the key to Sunday School growth. One of the best things a denomination or a church can do to assist its growth through the Sunday School, in my opinion, is to affirm and advocate that the pastor is the chief officer and head teacher of the local church's Bible teaching-reaching ministry. So long as a Sunday School is separated and distanced from the pastor, it may tend to be cut off from the church. I like the "hands-on" approach which this pastor and minister of education team advocate for the pastor in Sunday School evangelism.

You will like the apt illustrations in this book. These men write with a passion for winning the lost which bleeds through their manuscript. They are unapologetic evangelicals in their theological orientation, but they desire to make a contribution to the whole church. When these experienced growth leaders tell us how to grow an evangelistic Sunday School, they do not dogmatically insist that *their* way is the only way. Instead, they walk humbly with God and with us in this Abrahamic pilgrimage toward the Bible's new Jerusalem.

I plan to use this book as a textbook in my seminary course on Evangelism Through Church Organizations. Heretofore, we have had nothing quite like this text in print. Seminarians will relish it.

Without any hesitation or mental reservation I recommend *Growing An Evangelistic Sunday School* to all denominational executives, pastors, ministers of education, and Sunday School leaders and teachers who sincerely want to grow evangelistic churches through evangelistic Sunday Schools—and who want to practice holistic evangelism which is both wholesome and intelligent.

*Delos Miles*
*Professor of Evangelism*
*Southeastern Baptist Theological*
*Seminary*
*Wake Forest, North Carolina*

### Note

1. See Michael Green, *Evangelism in the Early Church* (Grand Rapids: William B. Eerdmans Publishing Co., 1970), 204.

# Contents

# 1
# Is the Sunday School Evangelistic?

"Preacher, you reach them, and we'll teach them!" In my early church experience this was a veritable refrain of Sunday School leaders. No one was being malicious or stubborn. The leaders were simply issuing a statement of their understanding of the division of duties. The pastor, or some hand-picked evangelism committee, was responsible for the outreach of the church, and the Sunday School leaders were responsible for Christian education once the prospects were reached and enrolled. Were they right or wrong? Should the Sunday School play a role in outreach? Is it designed, organized, or equipped for outreach? Should it be? Are the Sunday Schools in most of our churches evangelistic in nature?

## Personal Pilgrimage

Being the son of a Baptist pastor, I grew up in Southern Baptist organizational structure. I left college and attended The Southern Baptist Theological Seminary and then Cambridge University. I had a sure call from God, and I knew that I wanted to be a pastor. I wanted to be on the cutting edge of what God was doing through the church. I had strong personal convictions concerning the centrality of evangelism in the life of the church. I knew that God's desire is that none should perish. I was convinced that Christ alone was the way of redemption, and I must devote my best energies to communicating that message to a lost and needy world.

What I did not know was the best way to accomplish this task. Through my study of the Bible I had no doubt that the church, as the body of Christ, was the primary instrument through which God would redeem the world. I had devoted hours to the study of Matthew 16:16-19 in which Christ announced His intention of building His church. I projected myself back into that text and allowed the excitement of that revelation to become my own as if I were there with those first-century disciples. I gloried in this victorious pronouncement: "The gates of Hades shall not overpower it," and "I will give you the keys of the kingdom of heaven." I was awed and humbled by the reality that eternity itself was at stake in the activities of the church.

I hungered to know more about the power available to the church today. I thus immersed myself in Paul's Letter to the Ephesians because of its detailed focus on the church. As I studied the first chapter, Paul's prayer for the saints came alive to me. "I pray that the eyes of your heart may be enlightened, so that you may know what is the hope of His calling, what are the riches of the glory of His inheritance in the saints, and what is the surpassing greatness of His power toward us who believe" (1:18-19). It was as if Paul were praying this for me. "Look Ken, don't you understand what is available to and through the church. I have not altered my commission nor my promise to the church."

The key that opened the door for understanding was right there in the text. God's promises for the individual believer and for the church in accordance with the strength of His might (v. 19). God's might is then defined as the power that raised Jesus from the dead and seated Him at the right hand of the Father, far above all rule, authority, power, and dominion. I knew that the forgiveness of my sins and my personal redemption had been accomplished by the resurrection. I had personally witnessed this power at work in the transformation of the lives of repentant sinners. I had never doubted God's power to work in the individual life, but I had never really thought much about the power of His resurrection and the ministry of the church. The last two verses of that first chapter leapt from the page: "He put all things in subjection under His feet, and gave Him as head over all things to the church, which is His body, the fulness of Him who fills all in all" (1:22-23).

Was I to take this literally? Could the church truly express the fulness of God in the world today? I continued my journey through Ephesians. I could identify with Paul's wonder that he was privileged to preach the unfathomable riches of Christ to the Gentiles (3:8). I knew that same sense of wonder and amazement at being called to preach. When we truly comprehend the nature and task of the New Testament church, we are awed to play even a small part in its ministry. God's desire, Paul declared, was to make known the manifold wisdom of God to the rulers and authorities in the heavenlies *through the church* (3:10). God wants to demonstrate His wisdom through us! Once again Paul broke into prayer that believers would be strengthened in the inner man, that they would know the love of Christ and be filled to the fulness of God (3:14-19). Our task demands it! The world desires to see a people filled to the fulness of God. The good news is that we are able to fulfill God's expectation. Listen to the resounding benediction to this passage: **"Now to Him who is able to do exceeding abundantly beyond all that we ask or think, according to the glory in the church and in Christ Jesus to all generations forever and ever. Amen."**[1]

## Practical Experience

Nothing tests your theology like a good dose of practical experience. In February 1981, I became the pastor of First Baptist Church of Norfolk. God blessed my ministry with immediate response. People were joining the church every Sunday. We had very little staff and even less financial resources, so I did nothing but the basics: preach, teach, train, and visit. It was working, and the church quickly outgrew my practical knowledge. What do I do now? How do I care for the needs of the church members and keep reaching the lost? I knew God's promises of sufficiency were sure, but I needed some practical tools to organize the church.

Theologically, I was convinced that church growth and the nurturing of Christians was possible, yet, practically, I was a little shaky. I knew of so few churches who seemed to be making great strides at penetrating their own neighborhoods, and still caring for their own people, that I didn't know where to go for help. I met pastors who were disillusioned with their church and its potential to grow. They were nearly defeated. I talked with laypersons who desired to see something happen in their church, but had no idea how to get started. They saw the growth of our church and wanted help. Little did they know how desperately I was searching for a handle myself.

I began to add practical knowledge to my biblical convictions by reading books about church growth. I read Peter Wagner, C. B. Hogue, Charles Chaney and Ron Lewis, Donald McGavran, Winfield Arn, Delos Miles, Ron Jenson and Jim Stevens, Lewis Drummond, John Bisagno, and a host of others. I attended conferences on church growth, preaching, and prayer. I knew that any program devoid of prayer was useless. I talked with pastors who were reaching people. I learned immeasurably from all these sources and am still deeply indebted to all of them.

Yet I was still frustrated and unsure. There were many good ideas and various churches were obviously using these ideas successfully. I read and heard about cell groups meeting in homes, praise worship, novel approaches to organizing the church, different methodologies for structuring the evangelistic outreach of the church, and the megachurch approach. Some seemed to depend on the area of the country or the personality of the pastor. Which way should I go? I couldn't try them all—certainly not at one time. Some clearly would not work in our setting. For a while, I tried parts of various ideas but with limited success. I would announce a new program, kick it off, and then become disillusioned with it when it failed to produce according to my expectations. I knew my people must be getting frustrated by my apparent indecision. I found it difficult to adequately manage my time and energy so as to meet the daily ministry needs of the church, administer the existing organizations such as Sunday School, Church Training, mission groups, and so forth, and still plan and implement new growth programs. We were clearly doing *too much* with *too little* results. Was it possible to reach our community with the gospel, meet the personal needs of church members, and not neglect my family? Was there one simple plan?

I was at a stalemate! I have since discovered that many pastors and churches have come to this same point of frustration: you want to break out of the rut! You want to reach your community for Christ, but you just don't know which direction to take. I couldn't throw up my hands and do nothing. Too much was at stake!

## An Emerging Direction

A number of events converged in my own life at that time that helped give direction to my ministry. Our church participated in an association-sponsored church growth conference. I remember sitting in those meetings, led by Robert Stewart, taking copious notes. I was surprised to hear him use many of the key phrases and ideas that I had been reading in various church-growth books. I was surprised because he was talking about Sunday School as the growth organization of the church. I believed in Sunday School. I grew up in Sunday School. I had just never thought of Sunday School as the growth organization of the church. I had never seen it as the veritable spinal column of activity. I had certainly never thought of Sunday School and evangelism together.

During this same time I attended two different conferences that had a profound impact on my life. Our Sunday School director, Dick Baker, and I drove to Ridgecrest to attend a Growth Spiral Conference led by Andy Anderson, a growth specialist with the Baptist Sunday School Board. Andy got my attention one day when he asked if any of our churches needed more money to run the programs. We were hurting financially, and I needed any help I could get. Andy then shared the principle that giving followed attendance and that attendance was dictated by enrollment. All you had to do was to go out and enroll people through Sunday School. It all sounded so simple that it had to be too good to be true! If it worked so well, why wasn't everybody doing this?

If this guy could help me raise the level of our budget giving, I decided I would listen to the rest of the program. I was amazed that I was once again hearing ideas that I had read in church-growth books: (1) Find the people! (2) Provide the space! (3) Equip the leadership! (4) Enlarge the organization; (5) Divide and multiply. Sometimes different labels were used. For example, church-growth books often spoke of the pyramid principle for enlarging the organization. Yet, the parallels of thought were unmistakable. Suddenly, it dawned on me. *Why should I create all sorts of new organizations when I have an exciting organization that already embraces acknowledged church-growth principles: Sunday School? How have I missed this obvious connection between church growth and Sunday School?*

I left that conference with a clarity of vision concerning the vital role of Sunday School as the central organization for church growth, but I was still perplexed. If the Sunday School structure of my denomination embraces many of the recognized church-growth principles, why were so few churches growing?

The last piece of the puzzle was inserted at a conference where Harry Piland, director of the Sunday School Division, was the keynote speaker. In one of his sermons, Piland rocked the audience with the statement that if an adult Sunday School class had not attempted to lead anyone to Christ during the past year, it had forfeited its purpose for existing. Sunday School and evangelism! Our teachers were as shocked as I. Some returned wondering if they should resign their positions. I counseled them that they need not quit, but we all needed to repent and start with this new focus.

I don't know why, but I had never really connected Sunday School and evangelistic outreach. I suppose I agreed with those laypersons who said, "Preacher, you reach them, and we'll teach them." I have since discovered that few pastors, religious educators, or laypeople think of evangelism as a vital role of the Sunday School. They see Sunday School's primary task as nurturing Christians, not as reaching the unsaved. The commitment to outreach provides the vitality which energizes all the different facets of the Sunday School and enables them to function properly. Evangelism is the soul of the Sunday School! Without an emphasis on evangelism, the Sunday School loses its central focus, sinks to mediocrity, and simply struggles to maintain the status quo. However, when evangelism is given its rightful place as the focal point of the Sunday School, then we have the finest church-growth tool available today.

## A Historical Perspective

Was Sunday School intended to have evangelism at its center? An event from my childhood has placed this question in bold relief for me. When I was nine years old, my family moved from Morganton, North Carolina, across the state to Thomasville. It was a difficult move. We left a lovely new facility that was actually under construction when I was born. Our church in Thomasville was quite old and in disrepair. The church in Morganton was located on a lovely green hill, and the one in Thomasville overlooked a lumber yard. I couldn't understand my father's decision for moving our family to Thomasville. He obviously saw something that my boyish eyes couldn't.

The church soon began to grow, and the congregation voted to relocate about two miles away on a major thoroughfare. The site was purchased and work began. Dad often took me with him on daily inspections of the new site. One afternoon we arrived just after the footings for the new building had been poured. I walked behind Dad as we stepped over the strings and jumped the ditches laden with fresh concrete. My father could see the building as if it were already complete. "Here will be the foyer, the pulpit will be about here, and back here will be the baptistry." At that point he stopped, and he motioned with his hand to the land just being bulldozed behind the baptistry. "There's where the education building will be built." Perhaps it was the linking of the baptistry and the education building, I'm not sure, but I'll never forget what he said next. "I can remember when most of our baptisms came through the Sunday School. Not anymore! I lead most of the people to Christ now. Their loyalty is to the worship service and not Sunday School. Things have sure changed. It didn't use to be this way."

"Preacher, you reach them, and we'll teach them!"

I have been intrigued by that observation of my dad. "It didn't use to be this way." The value of the Sunday School as the focal point of evangelism and church growth has been a cardinal principle from its inception.

In 1902, E. Y. Mullins said: "The Sunday School must more and more prove a factor of power in the pastor's work. Already in many churches the Sunday School is the chief and almost only hope for church growth."

In 1911, J. M. Frost said:

> The school becomes as an agency what the church makes it; is capable of almost indefinite expansion in church efficiency as a channel for the output of its energy and life. . . . As a force for study and teaching the Word of God; as a force for evangelizing and bringing lost sinners to the Savior; as a force for instruction and education in the mightiest things claiming the attention of men, as a force for mission operation in the worldwide sense; as a force for making Christian character in men and women; and for opening the door of usefulness in a large scale—in all these things so essential in the life and mission of the church, the Sunday School holds rank among its very first and chosen agencies.[2]

In 1922, Arthur Flake wrote: "The supreme business of Christianity is to win the lost to Christ. This is what churches are for . . . surely then the Sunday School must relate itself to the winning of the lost to Christ as an ultimate objective." Flake listed as one of the standard requirements: "The school should be positively evangelistic."[3]

In 1934, in his excellent book *How to Win to Christ*, P. E. Burroughs brought together preaching and Sunday School in the work of evangelism, but he left little doubt what he saw as the primary work of the Sunday School.

> Winning to Christ holds central place in the Sunday School. Beyond all question the supreme business of the Sunday School is winning to Christ. . . . Failing here, we have failed utterly. It is of little avail that our youths shall grow up to know the Bible if they do not come to know by a vital expression the Christ of the Bible. . . . If the Sunday School fails in winning to Christ, it fails in its main business.[4]

In 1960, A. V. Washburn wrote:

> Until God's motive is our motive, his concern our concern, we will do little about the opportunities around us. . . . Two great convictions must literally dominate every Christian today—the multiplying millions of lost people that abound everywhere and the matchless power in Christ to transform them. . . . Here we stand before a host of unreached people, to lead them through Bible study to find Christ as Savior and Lord. Surely, we today feel acutely the responsibility of such a task and accept it as a burden of our souls.[5]

This focus on evangelism through the Sunday School has been echoed in more recent Sunday School writings. Harry Piland in 1980 wrote:

> The goal of our proclamation, witness, and ministry is to reach out to persons; to reach out on behalf of our Lord to the teeming masses of bewildered, frightened, hurt, confused, anxious, and lonely people. Our mission is *for* Christ, *in* love, and *to* persons.[6]

Max Caldwell in 1982 wrote: "The ultimate objective of a balanced program of Sunday School work is to win the lost to Christ. The ultimate objective of your church's Sunday School is to win the lost to Christ."[7]

We could add a host of others to the above selection. Without question we can conclude that, historically, the distinctive focus of the Southern Baptist Sunday School organization has been evangelism. Delos Miles has clearly pointed to evangelism through Sunday School as a contribution of Southern Baptists to church-growth thinking. In a brief tracing of the history of Southern Baptist Sunday School, Miles noted that evangelism has long been an article of faith among Southern Baptists. The distinct contribution of Southern Baptists was the focusing of evangelism in the Sunday School in such a manner that it was not simply a "children's affair" or a "teaching agency," but the "soul-winning enlistment agency of the local Southern Baptist Church."[8]

Max Caldwell agreed:

> Southern Baptists' approach to the use of the Sunday School is unique among the major denominations. The uniqueness has centered in our insistence on maintaining the Sunday School as the outreach-witnessing arm of the church.[9]

While we may well agree concerning our historical distinctive in this matter, we must ask a contemporary question: Are our Sunday Schools evangelistic? Max Caldwell warned:

> Just because the Sunday School has been an effective means of sharing God's Word in the past, however, doesn't necessarily make it so today. We cannot take the Sunday School for granted. We are less than one generation away from forgetting the purposes of Sunday School. If we ever fail to share with new people the purposes of Sunday School and the need to do effective Sunday School work, we could wake up one day to realize that our Sunday Schools have lost their zeal for reaching out to the lost world.[10]

### A Look at the Facts

Our stated purpose for Sunday School is growth through evangelism, but what do recent figures tell us? Nearly all church-growth experts emphasize the necessity of diagnostic research. If we ignore the statistical data we are doomed to mere feelings and speculations. Church-growth specialists look at the church-growth rates over a ten-year period. The relevant data is gathered for a ten-year period and placed on a chart. First the annual growth rates (AGR) are figured for each of the ten-years, and then the decadal growth rate (DGR) is calculated for the entire period.[11]

Several years ago I became very troubled by statistical data concerning my denomination. I was privileged to be at a Christian conference center in 1985 for a "Planned Growth in Giving" conference. In that conference I received a wonderful little book called *Cooperation: The Baptist Way to a Lost World*. I was disturbed by a chart that showed Southern Baptist growth for the period from 1940 to 1960 and then from 1960 to 1980. The years from 1940 to 1960 were designated the years of growth and expansion. They were our most exciting years as a denomination. Sunday School enrollment nearly doubled during those 20 years. A quick glance at the chart reproduced below will indicate that in most areas we have been marching in place since 1960.[12]

|  | 1940 | 1960 | 1980 |
|---|---|---|---|
| Number of Churches | 25,259 | 32,251 | 35,831 |
| Membership | 5,104,327 | 9,731,591 | 13,606,808 |
| Baptisms | 245,500 | 386,469 | 429,742 |
| S. S. Enrollment | 3,590,374 | 7,382,550 | 7,433,405 |
| Church Income | $40,359,038 | $480,108,902 | $2,483,645,000 |
| Cooperative Program | $3,415,124 | $48,689,694 | $207,471,751 |
| No. of State Conv. | 19 | 28 | 34 |
| Foreign Missionaries | 446 | 1,480 | 3,059 |
| Countries Served | 13 | 45 | 95 |

I wondered what would happen if we put our Southern Baptist Sunday School data under the scrutiny of diagnostic research. The following are the decadal growth figures for enrollment.

| 1940—1950 | 39.9 percent |
|---|---|
| 1950—1960 | 46.9 percent |
| 1960—1970 | 1.25 percent |
| 1970—1980 | 0.0134 percent |

We can at a glance notice the growth of the period 1940 to 1960, and the subsequent decline from 1960 to 1980. Wagner gives the following chart for evaluating decadal growth rates.

25 percent DGR—marginal growth
50 percent DGR—fair growth
100 percent DGR—good growth
200 percent DGR—excellent growth
300 percent DGR—outstanding growth
500 percent DGR—incredible growth

When looking at the above grading chart we must keep in view the vast size of the Southern Baptist Convention. I would rate the growth of the period of the 1940s-60s as good for a denomination of our magnitude. We must, nonetheless, view the negative figures for 1960-80 as cause for concern. To keep these figures in proper perspective I must point out that a majority of the mainline denominations suffered dramatic statistical declines beginning in the mid-1960s.[13] The most disturbing statistic on the chart relates to baptisms. The drop-off in the number of baptisms has been the most extreme of any statistic. The rate of baptisms per 100 members in 1975 was half that of 1950.[14]

For the sake of completeness we should bring our statistical data up-to-date. If we look at the DGR for the most recent ten-year period (1977-1987), we find that Sunday School enroll-ment grew by 6.75 percent. While the figure is not large, it may well suggest that we have turned the corner on the pe-riod of decline. Yet we must temper this with the fact that in 1987 Sunday School enrollment actually declined for the sec-ond time in a row after six years of gains. The 1987 church membership figure of 14,727,770 represented an increase of 109,203 members over 1986. Yet this was the smallest in-crease in church membership since 1936 and reflects a contin-uing slowdown in membership growth.[15] The present Church Training trend is down while the trend in baptisms remains level at 386,000. Baptisms have been at this level for 40 years. It is indeed disturbing that the greatest area of baptismal decline among Southern Baptists is found among the young adult category.[16] No baptisms were indicated by 7,244 of those churches reporting in 1987. A number 687 higher than 1986. Only 11,131 of the churches reporting conducted weekly visitation and only 5,398 have weekly workers' meetings.[17]

## Interpreting the Trend

It is one thing to gather statistics and quite another to explain them. No doubt there were numerous interrelated factors in the declining figures for a majority of the major denominations. Peter Wagner drew attention to the social upheavals of the 1960s and the subtle priority shift among the major denominations from the evangelistic mandate to the cultural mandate. Interestingly, Wagner observed that Southern Baptists did not participate in the tremendous decline because they continued to prioritize evangelism. After a closer look at the statistics we must question whether Wagner should have omitted Southern Baptists from those who had lost the focus of evangelism.

In *Leading Your Church to Growth,* Peter Wagner linked the shift from an emphasis on evangelism with the legacy of liberal theology.[18] Liberal theology dulls the desire for evangelism and prompts the shift of emphasis. Ralph Smith looked specifically at the declining Sunday School attendance in Southern Baptist life during the last two decades. He argued that the subtle shift from an emphasis on evangelism to education was the greatest contributing factor in our denominational decline.[19] Phillip Barron Jones in his chapter, "An Examination of the Statistical Growth of the Southern Baptist Convention" wrote: "In recent years the membership of the convention has become less evangelistic, or society is less receptive to its evangelistic efforts."[20] In response to Jones's conclusion we must note that the most recent Gallup report on worldwide trends in religion shows a renewed search for spiritual depth and a renewed search for more meaningful and spiritually based relationships. If it is true that people are searching, we must ask whether we have lost the focus—the very soul of our Sunday School. Our honest look at the statistics would not permit us to say that our Sunday Schools are evangelistic.

## Reversing the Trend

It is never easy to turn a declining situation around, whether it is in an individual church or in a denomination, but it can be done. It takes prayer, the empowering of the Holy Spirit, and a commitment to hard work. We can grow if we are willing to pay the price for reaching our communities for Jesus Christ. The signs of religious hunger are everywhere to be seen. Neither the commission of the church nor its source of empowering have been altered. The gospel is as relevant to the needs of contemporary humanity as at any other time in history. I believe that the opportunity exists for unparalleled growth in Sunday School attendance and baptisms. We must, however, recapture the clear focus on evangelism. The process has begun at the denominational level, but it must now be embraced by local churches all over our Convention. This book is dedicated to that end.

### Notes

1. Kenneth S. Hemphill, *The Official Rulebook for the New Church Game* (Nashville: Broadman Press, April 1990).
2. J. N. Barnett, *A Church Using Its Sunday School* (Nashville: The Sunday School Board of the Southern Baptist Convention, 1937), 17-18.
3. Arthur Flake, *Building a Standard Sunday School* (Nashville: The Sunday School Board of the Southern Baptist Convention, 1922), 106.
4. P. E. Burroughs, *How to Win to Christ* (Nashville: The Sunday School Board of the Southern Baptist Convention, 1934), 14-16.
5. A. V. Washburn, *Outreach for the Unreached* (Nashville: Convention Press, 1960).
6. Harry Piland, *Basic Sunday School Work* (Nashville: Convention Press, 1980), 13.
7. Max L. Caldwell, *A Guide to Standard Sunday School Work* (Nashville: Convention Press, 1982), 55.
8. Delos Miles, *Church Growth: A Mighty River* (Nashville: Broadman Press, 1981), 43.

9. Caldwell, 58.

10. Caldwell, 8 *ff.*

11. C. Peter Wagner, *Strategies for Church Growth* (Ventura: California, Regal Books, 1987), 161.

12. Cecil Ray and Susan Ray, *Cooperation: The Baptist Way to a Lost World* (Nashville: The Stewardship Commission of the Southern Baptist Convention, 1985), 36.

13. Dean R. Hogue and David A. Roozen, *Understanding Church Growth and Decline: 1950-1978* (New York: The Pilgrim Press, 1979), 144-159.

14. Ibid., 155,159.

15. James A. Lowry, "Research Information Report" *Denomination Statistics,* Series I, Number 1, March 1988.

16. 1987 SBC Statistics: Selected Highlights and Commentary, 10 February 1988.

17. James A. Lowry, "Research Information Report."

18. Peter Wagner, *Strategies*, 108-110.

19. C. Peter Wagner, *Leading Your Church to Growth* (Ventura: California, Regal Books, 1984), 33

20. Phillip Barron Jones, Chapter 7: "An Examination of the Statistical Growth of the Southern Baptist Convention." Dean R. Hoge and David A. Roozen, eds. *Understanding Church Growth and Decline* (New York: Pilgrim Press, 1979).

# 2
# Why Evangelism Must Be the Priority of Sunday School

Does it really matter if evangelism is the priority of the Sunday School at your church? Could you not do outreach another way and get equally satisfying results? Does every church need to be evangelistic? What if we feel called primarily to a discipling ministry? Can't we leave evangelism to the more aggressive churches? Precisely what is evangelism? Do we have to knock on doors and read a gospel tract to have an evangelistic Sunday School? All of these are vital questions and must be answered if we are going to experience renewed Sunday School growth.

## Defining Evangelism

You may be surprised to learn that there is an ongoing debate concerning the precise definition of evangelism. We need not resolve the subtleties of this matter, but we do need to develop a good working definition of evangelism. We cannot afford to be too vague. Sometimes "evangelism" is used loosely to describe virtually any activity done by the church. Therefore, every church could claim to be evangelistic. This is an inappropriate definition and leads to a meager harvest. It is essential that we be more precise in defining evangelism.

First, we should clarify that church growth is not to be confused with evangelism. There are three ways that churches grow. (1) *Biological growth* refers to that growth that occurs when the children of church members come of age and are thus assimilated into the life of the community. In my tradition this would be a form of evangelism since we believe a child must respond to the gospel and be saved before becoming a part of the church. Yet, if this is the full extent of our evangelism, we are clearly failing to fulfill the Great Commission. (2) The second method of growth is *transfer growth* which occurs when members from another church or denomination join our church. There are times when it looks like the churches in our area are playing fruit-basket turnover, resorting the converts. This is not evangelism. (3) *Conversion growth* is true evangelistic growth. It occurs when the gospel is shared, and someone is led to a saving knowledge of Christ and to responsible membership in the church.[1]

Christian leaders use "evangelism" in three primary ways today. *Presence evangelism* indicates that our primary witness to those outside the faith should be to do good works and help meet their needs. Persons who accept this definition reason that social action should be called "evangelism" whether it is done in the name of Christ or not. Although Christian presence is certainly critical, by itself it is an inadequate definition of evangelism.

Recently, I was privileged to have dinner with Carl F. H. Henry during the time we were both teaching a January course at The Southern Baptist Theological Seminary. At one point the table conversation turned to evangelism. Dr. Henry remarked that whatever definition of evangelism one selects it must, at the bare minimum, include a verbal declaration of the Evangel. Presence alone does not adequately define evangelism. It is an arrogant assumption on our part to believe that our actions are so thoroughly Christian they need no word of explanation. Even the Lord Jesus Himself combined word and deed in His witness. It is true that the salt of our life-style should make persons thirsty for the gospel, but it is equally true that the salt demands the light provided by a verbal witness. I would hasten to add that we cannot neglect the social aspects of the gospel in a comprehensive definition of biblical evangelism. Delos Miles has done a great service in his book *Evangelism and Social Involvement* (Broadman), in which he demonstrates that the social concern and evangelistic declaration must be held closely together.

*Proclamation evangelism* insists that a verbalization of the gospel must accompany good works. Once the proclamation has occurred and unbelievers have heard and understood the gospel, they are considered to be evangelized. A frequent motto of those who hold to this definition is "share Christ and leave the results to God." This is a very widely held view, and we must acknowledge that the results of evangelism are the work of the Holy Spirit alone. Nevertheless, we must wonder whether the proclamation definition sufficiently takes into consideration the command of our Lord to "Go out into the highways and along the hedges, and compel them to come in, that my house may be filled" (Luke 14:23). Is the proclamation definition sufficient in light of Paul's admonition in 2 Corinthians 5:20: "Therefore, we are ambassadors for Christ, as though God were entreating through us; we *beg you* on behalf of Christ, be reconciled to God" (my italics).

*Persuasion evangelism* goes a step beyond the presence and proclamation definitions. Persuasion evangelism does not consider a person to be evangelized until he or she responds to the good news of the gospel, becomes a disciple of Christ, and a responsible member of a local church. The persuasion definition best fits the command to "go therefore and make disciples" (Matt. 28:19-20) and the sense of urgency expressed in 2 Corinthians 5:20. Persuasion evangelism is not satisfied to think of evangelism as anything less than the making of disciples. True biblical evangelism involves a dual commitment to Christ and the church!

A persuasion definition was adopted by the Lausanne committee on evangelism toward the end of the 1970s. The definition was proposed by John Stott. "The nature of evangelization is the communication of the Good News. The purpose of evangelization is to give individuals a valid opportunity to accept Jesus Christ. The goal of evangelization is the persuading of men and women to accept Jesus Christ as

Lord and Savior, and serve Him in the fellowship of His church."[2]

Dr. Lewis Drummond defined evangelism in similar terms:

Evangelism is a concerted effort to confront the unbeliever with the truth about and claims of Jesus Christ and to challenge him with the view of leading him into repentance toward God and faith in our Lord Jesus Christ and, thus, into the fellowship of the church.[3]

Many of the great Sunday School men of my denomination have based their work on a persuasion definition of evangelism. P. E. Burroughs, for example, dealt thoroughly with the definition of evangelism in 1934. He selected the title *How to Win to Christ* for his book because it expressed the full-rounded task of evangelism. "Our real task is to win to Christ, to win and save the whole life though atoning grace, to redeem the whole being, all its elements and powers from sin to the kingdom and service of God."[4] The fact that Burroughs declared that our task is "to win" moves toward persuasion. He looked at the ultimate goal of evangelism as leading to service to God. Finally, his definition of evangelism involves the whole being.

The persuasion definition of evangelism best fulfills the biblical mandate for the church. It has the advantage of holding together conceptually what has traditionally been called *evangelism* and *follow-up*. It causes the church to integrate evangelism and social concern as we minister to the whole person. When embraced, it stimulates and leads to church growth. I believe that the Sunday School is the one organization best equipped to accomplish persuasion evangelism.

### Four Reasons to Make Evangelism the Primary Focus of Sunday School

#### We are Commissioned

The fact that we are commissioned to reach the world with the gospel should be enough reason for us to make it the focus of our Sunday Schools. The commission of the church is clearly stated in Matthew 28:19-20. The controlling thought of the verse is found in the imperative verb "make disciples." The methodology of the disciple-making process is found in the verbs *going, baptizing,* and *teaching.*

Often when I hear people speak of "making disciples," they actually mean the process of polishing Christians. Sometimes at growth conferences pastors will tell me that their church is not evangelistic. "They have chosen to emphasize discipleship," a pastor declares. Notice that the church is required to "go" in order to "make" disciples. The raw material from which the church makes disciples is unbelievers who need to commit their life to Christ, submit to baptism, and be taught all things.

The word *disciple*[s] occurs 269 times in the New Testament. Every occurrence is found in the Gospels and the Book of Acts, the books that deal with the initial establishment of the Christian movement. The first step in fulfilling the Great Commission requires that we persuade unbelievers to turn from sin and accept Jesus Christ as their personal Savior.

The task of evangelism is not complete when a mental or verbal assent is made to the proclamation of the gospel. The decision to follow Christ must be expressed through baptism. Baptism means more than simply getting an individual into a sufficiently large body of water to get them thoroughly wet. New Testament baptism has both individual and corporate elements. Not only does baptism demonstrate the incorporation of the person into the life of Christ, it also involves the incorporation of the new believer into Christ's body, the church. In 1 Corinthians 12:13 Paul reminded the divided Corinthian community: "For by one Spirit *we were all baptized into one body,* whether Jews or Greeks, whether slaves or free, and we were all made to drink of one Spirit" (my italics). This same theme is eloquently stated in Galatians 3:26-28: "For you are all sons of God through faith in Christ Jesus. For all of you who were baptized into Christ have clothed yourselves with Christ. There is neither . . . male nor female; for you are all one in Christ Jesus."

The story of Pentecost demonstrates both the individual and congregational aspects of baptism. Three thousand souls were added in one day (Acts 2:41). These souls were added individually because they had responded to Peter's message that they must: "Repent, and let each of you be baptized in the name of Jesus Christ for the forgiveness of your sins" (Acts 2:38). The corporate ramifications of baptism are expressed in Acts 2:42. "They were continually devoting themselves to the apostle's teaching and to fellowship, to the breaking of bread and to prayer." Biblical evangelism must lead to this step of full incorporation into the ongoing life of the body. God intended for children to be born into a full functioning family, both in the physical world and in the spiritual realm.

The Great Commission is brought into its full fruition when we teach those we have led to Christ to observe all that Jesus taught. This phrase looks at the lifelong process of Christian growth. The Great Commission demands that we put evangelism first. What organization in our church is better suited to fulfill the persuasion definition of evangelism than the Sunday School?

We must confess that evangelism is a thoroughly biblical activity. That in the midst of literally hundreds of good things we can do, it is the primary task of the church. We alone have been entrusted with the message that can bring unbelievers to saving faith in Christ.

## The Need of the Lost

A second factor that should motivate us to make evangelism the focus of our Sunday Schools is the need of the lost. Unless we have firm convictions about the eternal plight of persons outside of Christ, we will never be motivated to a strong focus on evangelism. We must believe that reconciliation to God in Christ is not something that makes life nicer or more palatable. Salvation is not something that will help one to be a better person, a better husband or wife. Reconciliation to Christ is life itself, without which there is *no hope*. A relationship to Christ is not merely preferable to unbelief or other forms of religious belief. A relationship to Christ leads to abundant life now and assures a heavenly home.

If we are going to restore evangelism to its proper place in our Sunday Schools, we must believe that (1) human beings without Christ are really lost (2) that hell is their eternal destiny, and (3) that we alone have the message of hope. Ralph Smith stated: "Great churches and Sunday Schools are built· out of a spirit of compassion for the unsaved."[5] Once we fully comprehend the condition of the unsaved, we must be moved with compassion to save them from their plight.

For a month in 1988, our nation's attention was riveted on the plight of three stranded whales. They were imprisoned by ice that threatened their lives. The response to their plight was overwhelming. Volunteers made heroic efforts to free the whales from their frigid entrapment. Under adverse circumstances, at the risk of their own lives, the volunteers worked day after day to free the whales. The crisis created a spirit of cooperation rarely seen today as Soviet icebreakers steamed to join the rescue effort. The world looked on in awe as these people were driven by their efforts to free the whales.

A few years ago, I witnessed similar heroic efforts as dead and dying dolphins began to wash ashore on Virginia beaches. Volunteers committed hundreds of man-hours, thousands of dollars were raised, and a community was stirred and united by their efforts to save the dolphins. I have nothing against whales or dolphins, but I place higher value on persons. Our Sunday Schools will flourish once more when we are moved by the plight of lost men and women, trapped in the icy tombs of sin, facing certain death and eternity separated from God. Our compassion for their plight will compel us to rescue them. Then the heartbeat of Sunday School—evangelism—will bring revival.

### Most Effective Means to Fulfill Great Commission

I believe that Sunday School provides for the church the single most effective means of accomplishing the Great Commission. This is by no means a new idea. Nearly 67 years ago

This is only when "open enrollment" is practiced

Arthur Flake gave four reasons that the Sunday School provided churches with the most commanding opportunity for soul-winning

- Large numbers of lost people are to be found in the Sunday School membership.
- The taught people belong to the Sunday School.
- Those who are most susceptible to the gospel message belong to the Sunday School.
- The soul-winners of a church are found in the Sunday School.[6]

I am continually amazed at the striking similarities between basic Sunday School work and church growth methodology. I am, however, no longer amazed at the contemporary relevance of the basics of Sunday School work. We must renew our commitment to the basics. Let me share seven reasons that shows the Sunday School to be the most effective *modern* tool for biblical evangelism.

(1) *The Sunday School provides the most natural and fertile field for evangelism.* A. V. Washburn reported that "in most churches 85 to 95 percent of those saved come through the Sunday School."[7] While the percentage may be lower today, we can hardly ignore the wisdom of our fathers. We must first consider the unsaved persons who are presently enrolled as priority candidates for the gospel. It was a foregone conclusion with Flake, Burroughs, Barnette, and other writers that unsaved persons would be enrolled in Sunday School. They often wrote of the children and the youth, but they also believed that unsaved adults were enrolled in Sunday School. Although a virtual consensus exists today that unsaved children are on Sunday School rolls, many persons are defensive about putting unsaved adults on the rolls. I have heard adult Sunday School teachers boast that there is not a single unsaved person on their rolls. I am delighted for them if this means they have personally shared the gospel with all their members. But I would ask, "Why stop now if you're having

such excellent results? Go out and enroll more unsaved
friends, so they too might have the gift of eternal life."

I am afraid that we have ignored the genuine evangelistic
prospects that exist among the inactive church members in
our Sunday School rolls. If true evangelism results in a dual
commitment to Christ and His church, then we still have
work to do.

The Sunday School also provides the natural field for evangelism because of the network of social connections that exist
between Sunday School members and unsaved persons in the
community. I am concerned that we have lost the vision for
enrolling the unsaved. Kennedy Smartt, a Presbyterian pastor, recently discovered the outreach possibilities of Sunday
School. He gives Southern Baptists the credit for his discovery. He believes that the unique evangelistic feature of Southern Baptist Sunday School is their open-door policy—anyone
can belong. Kennedy Smartt expressed mild surprise that
people come when invited. Many Sunday Schools, he observed, are designed to serve the "select of the elect," and
evangelistic outreach is the furthest thing from their minds.[8]
Are we in danger of neglecting opportunities for evangelism
through our Sunday Schools which other denominations are
just beginning to discover? The Sunday School provides the
link with our communities through existing personal relationships. Church-growth specialists frequently point out
that the most natural and receptive field for evangelism are
the fringes of an existing church. Win Arn, for example,
found, in the Billy Graham crusade in Seattle, that 83 percent
of those who made decisions and were incorporated in
churches one year later had friends or relatives already in
those churches.[9] The network of the Sunday School is the crucial key to effective evangelism.

(2) *Sunday School provides the proper atmosphere for effective and natural evangelism.* Church-growth writers speak of
body evangelism, friendship evangelism, and relational evangelism. All of these terms point to the concern for the dual
commitment to Christ and the church. Many churches have

adopted parachurch forms, methodology, and training for the evangelistic outreach program of the local church. The emphasis of most of the parachurch methodologies is on an intense one-on-one confrontation. The parachurch materials usually offer outstanding information on how to communicate the content of the gospel, but they are frequently weak on the task of assimilating new believers into the church. Many pastors and churches become disillusioned when large numbers of conversions are reported with a confrontation methodology, but little visible results are seen through the church or in the life of the believer. If, however, we adopt a definition of evangelism that requires us to follow through to the integration of the new believer in the life of the church, we cannot be satisfied with "verbal" decisions. We must see evangelism as a process that includes conviction, conversion, and maturation in the body of Christ.

Ron Jensen and Jim Stevens have an excellent discussion on the biblical nature of evangelism. They wrote:

> In reading the New Testament we have the impression that evangelism was a spontaneous by-product of natural process within the church. People were attracted because something in the body was attractive. People saw what took place in the corporate life of the church, and saw how the believers responded to the external pressure which constantly faced the church. We suspect that an organized, structured evangelism "program" with a full-time specialist would have been out of place. Evangelism in the New Testament was not so much "done" as it was "occurring." . . . Evangelism would spring from *koinonia*. There would be a magnetism about a body of people who love each other.

Jenson and Stevens conclude that "evangelism today has lost its naturalness and spontaneity. It is a struggle. It is programmed and structured. Most people feel guilty for not evangelizing."[10]

We have in Sunday School the proper climate to restore the naturalness of the audiovisual aspects of true evangelism. Here we can combine training in sharing the gospel with personal relationships. Here the results of confrontational evangelism can be conserved.

(3) *Sunday School provides for the involvement of laypersons.* Most writers in the field of evangelism declare that the training and use of laypersons is the key to world evangelization. Dr. Lewis Drummond wrote: "May I be bold and at the very outset state quite categorically that unless the church recaptures and implements the principle of a lay-centered ministry, I see little hope of fulfilling the commission to evangelize our day."[11] Again the Sunday School provides the greatest tool for the training and involvement of large numbers of laypersons.

(4) *Sunday School provides the organizational structure to support body evangelism.* We have noted that the Sunday School class provides the natural atmosphere for both the audio and visual aspects of spontaneous evangelism to occur. This does not negate the need for an organization to support the entire system of body evangelism, the Sunday School organizational structure is the backbone of the evangelistic Sunday School. Spontaneity and structure are not mutually exclusive, but are in reality dependent on one another. Wayne Jones wrote: "The Sunday School is uniquely organized to reach people of all ages."[12]

(5) *The Sunday School focuses on the primary tool of evangelism—the Bible.* The Bible is the textbook of the Sunday School and the primary tool of evangelism. Paul wrote to Timothy concerning "the sacred writings which are able to give you the wisdom that leads to salvation through faith which is in Christ Jesus" (2 Tim. 3:15). Paul spoke of the gospel as the very power of God unto salvation in Romans 1:16. We are familiar with the promise of God in Isaiah 55:10-11 that His Word would not return void. Yet we are often guilty of giving only lip service to this biblical truth. If we were truly convinced of the power of the written and spoken Word of God, we would be doing more to enroll the unsaved in our Sunday Schools. Men like P. E. Burroughs and J. N. Barnette wrote about the role of the Bible in evangelism. Burroughs dedi-

cated a chapter to "using the Bible" in evangelism,[13] and Barnette entitled his third chapter "The Sunday School and Bible Evangelism."[14] Both chapters are well worth the reading.

(6) *Sunday School provides for the assimilation of new converts.* Evangelism by our persuasion definition is not complete until we lead people to a growing understanding of their commitment to Christ and the church. The Sunday School is certainly the most effective tool for this final step of evangelism. C. Peter Wagner underlined the importance of assimilating new believers into a small-group context. He cited studies that indicate those persons who will ultimately become active church members must identify an average of seven new friends within the first six months. Wagner argued that the assimilation process begins before conversion. The friendship of non-Christians with members of the church is the most important factor in eventual assimilation. He urged church members to form a close relationship with one or more non-Christians.[15] Wagner gave convincing statistics that should cause us to make this a priority. Seventy percent of those persons who are now active church members came to their personal faith and their involvement in a church through a member who saw the persuasive process of evangelism as relational. On the other hand, the dropout rate for those making decisions through confrontational evangelism alone is 90 percent. The Sunday School provides the essential tool for conserving results and assimilating new Christians. These facts and others have prompted our church to merge our entire outreach program with our Sunday School ministry.

George Gallop, in a speech to the Lausanne Committee for World Evangelization in 1987 agreed with the importance of the small group in disciple making. "Efforts to evangelize the world need to be directed first and foremost, of course, toward bringing to Christ followed by encouragement to join a Bible study or prayer fellowship group—a spiritual support group if you will—so that their spiritual life can be nurtured in a love relationship with others empowered by the Holy Spirit."[16]

(7) *Sunday School provides for the continuous cycle of disci-*

*ple making.* Disciple making must be an integral part of the ongoing life of the church. New Christians often have a large network of non-Christian friends. They can effectively reach their non-Christian friends through the Sunday School. They can initiate the relational process of evangelism even before they have any formal evangelistic training. If they bring them to their Sunday School class, the ongoing process has begun. Sunday School provides our greatest opportunity to reach the lost multitudes in every generation.

We are thoroughly committed to evangelism through the Sunday School at First Baptist, Norfolk. We use various training methodologies including Evangelism Explosion and Lay Evangelism School, yet our outreach visitation is organized through the Sunday School. Our goal is to staff every class with a trained evangelism outreach leader. Thus we will capitalize on the excellent training methodologies provided by some of the confrontational evangelism tools with the body fellowship of the Sunday School.

Furthermore our follow-up for new Christians is designed to be accomplished through the Sunday School and its partner: Church Training. Wayne will discuss this more thoroughly in chapter 10.

## Evangelism Gives Life to the Entire Sunday School Program

We have thus far focused around the question "Why evangelism must be the priority of Sunday School" in terms of its effectiveness in reaching the lost. There is one final matter that should not be overlooked. I would like for you to consider five reasons why evangelism gives life to the entire Sunday School program.

(1) *Evangelism restores enthusiasm to every aspect of the Sunday School program.* I could not possibly express this idea as eloquently as P. E. Burroughs who wrote:

A vision of the meaning of evangelism and an experience of the joys that come from winning the lost world transform many a Sunday School. Is it difficult to find among the great numbers of cultivated men and women in our churches those who will teach and bear the burdens of Sunday School? Do those who teach lack joyful and triumphant zeal? Let the fires of evangelism burn, let the community be pervaded by a quiet gracious revival, let the workers get a vision of the meaning and matchless dignity of what we are doing, as these things touch life and destiny, and all will be changed.[17]

Nothing will ignite the Sunday School like visible evangelistic results. Seeing the hand of God working through the Sunday School will infuse pastor and lay worker alike with new strength and resolve for the work of the Kingdom.

(2) *Evangelism creates natural and positive church growth.* In their book *Ten Steps for Church Growth,* Donald McGavran and Winfield Arn have a chapter entitled "Churches Grow as Priorities are Given to Effective Evangelism."[18] Ralph Smith pointed to the obverse of that truth in his observation that when churches cease to emphasize evangelistic outreach they cease to grow.[19]

C. B. Hogue presented a forceful biblical and practical case for the necessity of growth through evangelism. "Although its reason for witnessing is not self-motivated, to survive in the world, the church must grow. It must be propagative, the life of the church and its hope for the future lie in its reproductive power."[20] Without this central focus on evangelism, church growth itself loses its very foundation. It is therefore not too dramatic to say that the life of the church, and perhaps our denomination, depends on evangelistic Sunday Schools.

(3) *Evangelism defeats spiritual elitism.* There is a natural tendency for any group to become self-centered and ingrown. *Koinonia* can quickly degenerate in mere *cliquishness.* When the topic of Sunday School growth is addressed, one overriding concern is for the class that won't move, won't promote, and won't cooperate because of their "good" fellowship. The class that has lost its vision for the unsaved cannot experience biblical fellowship. A Sunday School with a focus on aggressive evangelism will go a long way toward curing the problem of spiritual elitism.

(4) *Evangelism gives a clear focus to the Sunday School and the church.* When we are not sure of our priorities or goals, we drift aimlessly from emphasis to emphasis. We tend to operate from the squeaky-wheel principle. We often spend our budget and our time on those programs that exert the strongest lobbying pressure. When Sunday School adopts the command to make disciples as its number-one goal it will have clear purpose.

(5) *Evangelism is the soul of the Sunday School program.* If the Sunday School is going to provide the backbone for the church's ministry, it must be continually nurtured by the life-giving nature of evangelism. Every Christian loves to hear a moving testimony of soul-winning. We want to give time and money to those ministries that are seeing evangelistic results. Evangelism is the spark of life that keeps the Sunday School functioning day after day, week after week, and year after year.

In the first chapter we posed the question: "Are our Sunday Schools evangelistic?" Historically, our Sunday Schools had clearly been evangelistic, but recent statistics suggest we are in danger of losing that clear focus. Here is an even more relevant question: "Is your Sunday School evangelistic?"

Max Caldwell listed seven questions to help answer this question.[21] Take the test!

- How many unreached persons, who are prospects for your class or department, can be identified right now?
- What actions are being taken by the class or department to cultivate persons not yet enrolled in Sunday School?
- Are unreached persons given an opportunity to enroll in your Bible-study group?
- What actions are being taken to support unsaved persons who are new enrolled in Bible study?
- Is prayer for unsaved persons practiced?
- Is the Bible teaching directed toward unsaved persons?
- Are class members actively witnessing to unsaved persons?

## Notes

1. C. Peter Wagner, *Strategies for Church Growth* (Ventura, Calif.: Regal Books, 1987), 115.

2. Wagner, *Strategies*, 113-130.

3. Lewis A. Drummond, *Leading Your Church in Evangelism* (Nashville: Broadman Press, 1975), 21.

4. P. E. Burroughs, *How to Win to Christ* (Nashville: The Sunday School Board of the Southern Baptist Convention, 1934), 13.

5. Ralph M. Smith and Bob Edd Shotwell, *Helping Churches Grow* (Nashville: Broadman Press, 1986), 28.

6. Arthur Flake, *Building a Standard Sunday School* (Nashville: The Sunday School Board of the Southern Baptist Convention, 1922), 107-110.

7. A. V. Washburn, *Outreach for the Unreached* (Nashville, Convention Press, 1980), 13.

8. Kennedy Smartt, "Evangelism Through Sunday School," *Pastor Evangelist*, ed. Roger S. Greenway (Phillipsburg, N.J.: Presbyterian and Reformer Publishing Co., 1987), 110-111.

9. Delos Miles, *Church Growth: A Mighty River* Nashville: Broadman Press, 1981), 127.

10. Ron Jensen and Jim Stevens, *Dynamics of Church Growth* (Grand Rapids, Mich.: Baker Book House, 1981), 188.

11. Lewis A. Drummond, *Leading Your Church in Evangelism* (Nashville: Broadman Press, 1975), 59-60.

12. R. Wayne Jones, *Overcoming Barriers to Sunday School Growth* (Nashville: Broadman Press, 1987), 28.

13. P. E. Burroughs, *How to Win to Christ*, 74-80.

14. J. N. Barnette, *Church Using its Sunday School* (Nashville: Sunday School Board of the Southern Baptist Convention, 1937), 49-64.

15. C. Peter Wagner, *Church Growth: State of the Art* (Wheaton, Ill.: Tyndale House Publishers, 1986), 64-65.

16. George Gallop, *Worldwide Trends in Religion*, 17. Speech given at Biennial Meeting of the Lausanne Committee for World Evangelization, Callaway Gardens, Georgia, 22 January 1987.

17. P. E. Burroughs, *How to Win to Christ*, 18.

18. Donald A. McGavran and Winfield C. Arn, *Ten Steps for Church Growth* (New York: Harper and Row, 1977), 51-60.

19. Ralph Smith and Bob Edd Shotwell, *Helping Churches Grow*, 29.

20. C. B. Hogue, *I Want My Church to Grow* (Nashville: Broadman Press, 1977), 23.

21. Max Caldwell, *A Guide to Standard Sunday School Work* (Nashville: Convention Press, 1982), 61-63.

# 3
# Removing the Blinders

If Sunday School truly is an effective tool, why is my denomination in a statistical holding pattern? Why have baptisms shown a flat growth curve for nearly 40 years? Why did we suffer 20 years of negative Sunday School enrollment growth? Why did the tool not work? The Sunday School is a growth tool; and, like any other tool, it must be properly used in order to produce satisfactory results.

Perhaps I can illustrate our dilemma with a personal confession. I am a sucker for the tool section of Sears. I love to walk up and down the aisles looking at the various tools and imagine what I could build or repair if I had the right tools. I'm an eclectic person. I like both the mechanical and the woodworking tools. Occasionally, I will buy a particular tool or even a small set of tools that I *really* need. One year my father-in-law gave me a lovely toolbox and an entire set of socket wrenches, open-end wrenches, and screwdrivers. On another occasion, I felt really generous toward myself and bought a few of the basic woodworking tools. I have a serious problem: I rarely use any of my tools. In many instances, I don't know how to use them. Sometimes, I'm just too lazy to learn. Occasionally I do clean out the garage and my toolbox. I wipe down my tools and neatly reorganize them in the toolchest. I still have a fond affection for my tools. But thus far I haven't consistently used any of them.

I've tried to analyze my mental block concerning the use of my tools. I'm not sure if I'm afraid that I can't learn to use them or that I can. Maybe I'm not able to learn to use these tools. They look awfully complicated. If I tried and failed, I might be discouraged. What if I could learn to use them successfully? My wife might want me to keep up the good work. She could think of a lot of nifty projects. I'm not sure that I want to work with my tools that much.

I wonder if my dilemma with tools and many churches' dilemma with Sunday School growth don't have a great deal in common? It is easy to collect and admire tools rather than use them. We can amass a great number of diplomas, badges, and buttons for our collection without ever truly using the knowledge and skills they represent. Sometimes we collect a new idea and we're afraid to try it lest we fail. At other times, we're afraid to try because we fear success. We fear the hard work that success can entail. Many pastors and Sunday School leaders have negative blinders when it comes to growth. These blinders are unfounded fears. It is much more critical that we remove these blinders when it comes to using our Sunday School to reach people than it is for me to use my tools. We have a lost world waiting to hear the gospel. We can look out on our communities with the eyes of Jesus and see fields that are ripe unto harvest.

## Previous Lists

The listing of growth barriers is nothing new. Virtually any church growth or Sunday School growth book will include such a list. Wayne Jones has devoted an entire book to identifying and overcoming barriers to Sunday School growth.[1] C. Peter Wagner, in his book *Your Church Can be Healthy*, diagnosed eight church diseases, two of which he said can be fatal.[2] Delos Miles in his book, *Church Growth: A Mighty River,* divided the obstacles to growth into three major classes: attitudinal, theological, and ecclesiastical. Attitudinal obstacles Miles listed include the following:

• It's up to them. The passive congregation expects people to come if they simply unlock the church doors.
• Numbers are unimportant. Faithfulness is the important thing.

- Small is beautiful. The corollary is that big is bad.
- Any change is to be resisted.
- America is overchurched.
- Denominations are evil.
- The unprintable signs. The body language of the congregation assures the visitor he or she is unwelcome.

Miles's listing of theological obstacles are also worthy of careful and prayerful attention.

- Sin. Sins such as showing partiality, divisions, stife, and immorality in the fellowship are sins that are particularly harmful to church growth.
- Planning for growth is unspiritual. The unfounded fear is that planning usurps the sovereignty of God.
- A lack of balance between the sovereignty of God and the freedom and responsibility of humanity.
- Paying lip service to the priesthood of believers.[3]

Kennedy Smartt listed apathy, lack of urgency, lack of purpose, lack of pastoral leadership and support and the power of tradition as the major obstacles to growth.[4] Ron Jensen, president of church dynamics, and Jim Stevens, pastor of membership development at the Church of the Savior in Wayne, Pennsylvania, listed: known sin, lack of desire to grow, lack of commitment to prayer, lack of leadership development, and extreme forms of church government as the diseases that stop church growth.[5]

I have no desire to attempt to develop an exhaustive list of negative blinders. If you simply compiled the suggestions mentioned above, you would have a lengthy list. Perhaps I can make a contribution for those of you who desire to build an evangelistic Sunday School by listing the most frequent responses I hear from pastors and Sunday School leaders.

## We'll Lose Our Fellowship

My list has not been arranged in any order of frequency, but in this case I have begun with the loss of fellowship because it is the first, and most frequent, concern expressed in conferences I have attended.

There can be little question that true biblical fellowship must be a high priority for any and every church. There is a hunger for fellowship in our day that makes church fellowship a matter of vital concern. If our churches do not provide opportunities for real fellowship, then the people of our communities will go elsewhere and substitute the artificial for the real. The proliferation of clubs, societies, and even bars speaks to the human need to discover fellowship. It is my conviction that the church alone has the potential to provide genuine fellowship, thus we cannot afford to sacrifice fellowship.

The Bible certainly speaks to the matter of fellowship. The Greek work *koinōnia*, "to have in common," is used frequently in the New Testament to picture Christian fellowship. Fellowship is more than coziness, it is a depth of sharing that involves the total person. One can hardly overlook the depth of sharing in the early church pictured in Acts:

> They were continually devoting themselves to the apostles' teaching and to fellowship, to the breaking of bread and to prayer. And everyone kept feeling a sense of awe; and many wonders and signs were taking place through the apostles. And all those who believed were together, and had all things in common; and they began selling their property and possessions, and were sharing them with all, as anyone might have need. And day by day continuing with one mind in the temple, and breaking bread from house to house, they were taking their meals together with gladness and sincerity of heart (Acts 2:42-46).

Who wouldn't long to experience true *koinonia?* But do we have to give up fellowship if we embrace outreach? Are they mutually exclusive? Let me answer from both the biblical the practical vantage points with a resounding *no*. Look back at the context of our Acts passage, if you will. In the verse just prior to where I began my quotation, we are told that "there were added that day about three thousand souls" (2:41). In the verse immediately following our passage we read "The Lord was adding to their number day by day those who were being saved" (2:47).

Let me make two observations. *True fellowship will actually create growth*. The world is so hungry for fellowship that when people find it in a church family, they will flock to that place. Each month my wife and I invite new church members into our home to welcome them to the church. We frequently have as many as 50 or 60 persons attending. I go around the room and ask them why they came to First Baptist. The overwhelming reason given is because of the fellowship they found in our church.

A second observation is that *numbers will not dilute fellowship*. We saw that very clearly in Acts 2. Numbers may cause you to lose some measure of comfort or coziness. It may cause you to break up cliques and create new Sunday School classes. C. Peter Wagner coined the word *koinonitis* from the Greek koinōnia to describe fellowship that has become diseased. Christian people enjoy each other's company so much they lose the vision for reaching the unchurched.[6] The only barrier to fellowship that I have discovered in the New Testament church is unconfessed and unforgiven sin. First John 1 speaks clearly to this matter. In studying the text you will notice several interesting facts. Fellowship is actually created by outreach and by the proclamation of the gospel (v. 3). Fellowship is hindered when we say that we have fellowship with God and yet sin (v. 6). Fellowship is healed when we confess our sins (v. 7).[7]

The Sunday School provides the tool that enables you to maintain quality fellowship while you reach your community. When you follow the proper procedure of creating new units in order to ensure small-group interaction, people will have the opportunity for intimate fellowship. Our commitment to fellowship recently led us to launch 70 new teaching units on the first day of the year. Outreach and growth will not cause you to lose the intimacy of fellowship.

### We'll Get Caught Up in the Numbers Game

The matter of "numbers" is often mentioned with the implied assumption that numbers are inherently bad, and churches that emphasize evangelism and growth are simply on an ego trip. There's no denying that all of us need to continually be aware of our motives and attitudes in ministry. The problem of ego can infect us in many areas, not just that of numbers.

Nonetheless, in many quarters there seems to be a literal aversion to numbers. You might be interested to know that the Sunday School writers of a generation ago did not share the modern-day aversion to numbers. Arthur Flake wrote:

There is inspiration in numbers. . . . However no Sunday School is worthy of being called a great Sunday School unless it is reaching a large majority of the people who should attend it. . . . a Sunday School must be reaching the people in a large way before being entitled to recognition as a Standard School.ᴬ

J. N. Barnette had three subtopics under his section on reaching people that he entitled: "God is for Numbers," "Jesus is for Numbers," and "Jesus Commands the Churches to Go after Numbers."[9] P. E. Burroughs's remark concerning numbers was pointed:

We do well as Sunday School workers to face quietly and faithfully the question as to what in the work of the school shall hold first and commanding place in our thinking. We make much of *numbers*. We bend unremitting efforts to enlarge our attendance. This we ought to do; we cannot teach people until we have first reached them.[10]

A. V. Washburn has a chapter entitled "MORE is the Word." He began that chapter: "The question has been raised by some, perhaps with an element of the critical in it, 'when will Southern Baptists get over this obsession with numbers?'"[11]

Since the aversion to numbers could keep us from obedience to our evangelistic task, we must seek to overcome this objection from a biblical and practical perspective. The fourth Book of the Bible is entitled Numbers, and even a cursory reading of that book will reveal that it is about *numbers*. God commanded Moses to number all of Israel (Num. 1:1-2). God was concerned for the safety and protection of Israel as they journeyed to the Promised Land. Some persons want to counter this passage by a reference to 1 Chronicles 21:1 where Satan moved David to number Israel. David's numbering of Israel, in this instance, was an issue of military pride, not pastoral care.

Numbering is a tool. As such it is neither inherently good or bad. It depends on the motive of the one doing the numbering. We do need to be careful when we use numbers for boasting, whether it involves numbers in Sunday School attendance or an amount given to the Cooperative Program or even the number of wins recorded by our church softball team. We shouldn't, however, reject the tool because it can be abused.

A quick glance at the New Testament provides ample evidence that numbers were considered by the Lord Jesus and the early church to be of vital significance. I have heard the objection that "Jesus told Peter to feed his sheep, not count them." Such a remark demonstrates both a lack of knowledge about shepherding and a lack of fairness in biblical interpretation.

Phillip Keller, a professional sheep rancher, wrote a book entitled: *A Shepherd Looks at Psalm 23*. Keller wrote that it is "essential for a careful shepherd to look over his flock every day, counting them to see that all are able to be up and on their feet."[12] We would do well to recall that Jesus told the parable of the man who had a hundred sheep, and one went astray (Luke 15). The only way to know the number of sheep in the fold is to count. Numbers in the Scripture are used both in terms of pastoral care and growth. Jesus spoke of a yield of 30, 60, and 100 fold. A small grain harvest is never characterized as beautiful. In Matthew 9:35-38 Jesus, seeing the *multitude* of people, told the disciples that the harvest was plentiful. Thus the command: "Therefore beseech the Lord of the harvest to send out workers into His harvest."

I find it fascinating that when John recorded the postresurrection fishing miracle at the Sea of Tiberias he told us there were 153 fish (John 21:11). I'm not a fisherman, but I assume that 153 fish are better than 100 or even 152. God had no aversion to keeping records. He told us that the hairs of our heads are numbered (Luke 12:6-7). If records of hairs, fish, and sheep are important, how much more vital are the records of people?

The Book of Acts literally bristles with references to numbers and growth. I will list just a few to entice you to look further into the Book of Acts. All italics are mine.

- 1:15—"A gathering of about *one hundred and twenty persons was there together.*"
- 2:41—"There were added that day about *three thousand souls.*"
- 2:47b—"The Lord was *adding to their number* day by day those who were being saved."
- 4:4—"The number of the men came to be about *five thousand.*"
- 5:14—"All the more believers in the Lord, *multitudes* of men and women, were constantly *added to their number.*"
- 6:1—"Now at this time while the disciples were increasing in *number.*"
- 6:7—"The *number* of the disciples continued to increase greatly in Jerusalem, and a *great many* of the priests were becoming obedient to the faith."
- 11:21—"The hand of the Lord was with them, and a *large number* who believed turned to the Lord."
- 11:24—"*Considerable numbers* were brought to the Lord."
- 11:26—"They met . . . and taught *considerable* numbers; and the disciples were first called Christians in Antioch."

Perhaps some persons object to numbers because they are concerned about superficial commitment, padding the rolls, and the deceitful inflation of numbers. I share those concerns. Others object to numbers because they want to use their objection as a smoke screen to cover up their genuine lack of concern for the lost people in their community and the inactive people on their rolls. They are afraid they may have to work if they get this tool out of their closely guarded toolbox.

Numbering our people is a God-given tool. Good records are a must for any Sunday School that cares about reaching the lost and ministering to the saved. Numbers are helpful both in pastoral care and evangelism.

## We'll Forfeit Our Quality

This concern is expressed both in terms of quantity versus quality and faithfulness versus success. Again we must confess that the emphasis on quantity can be harmful if it is an unbalanced emphasis. We have certainly witnessed the abuse of the success motive in our day. But the abuse of quantity and success should not cause us to jettison our concern for the multitudes. There are those who point to 1 Corinthians 4:2 with the emphasis that God is concerned with faithfulness and not success. But we would do well to balance this verse with the parable of the talents where the master rewards the successful investment of the talents. Faithfulness and successfulness are not opposites when it comes to servants of Christ.

J. N. Barnette leveled a rather stinging rebuke at those who want to see quantity and quality as opposites. "Such expressions as it is not numbers that count, but quality, may have some truth, but not all the truth. Sometimes leaders place quality against numbers. The statement, I had rather have a good Sunday School than a big one, comes from a heart that has been deceived by the forces of evil, from a heart of indifference, or from a heart that is seeking to cover failure with pious platitudes."[13]

It is not a matter of either/or. We can maintain quality and quantity. The truth of the matter is that true quality will produce quantity. We have witnessed this in the business world. The old adage concerning building a better mousetrap works in the realm of church growth. A quality Sunday School with proper balance will have such a warm fellowship, a strong organization, and an effective outreach program that it will produce quantity. If your Sunday School is not producing any quantitative growth, you need to take a careful look at the quality of the program. A healthy, living organism will grow by the nature of its good health. It should exhibit the properties of a living organism. Your Sunday School can and should grow.

## We'll Lose Control

"If the church grows and new people come in, I won't be needed." Existing leaders sometimes fear that growth will put them out of a job. Two things are worth mentioning. First, a growing Sunday School requires a large reservoir of leaders. To provide for the quality of the Sunday School, proper teaching ratios must be maintained. A growing Sunday School will never put a person out of work. Second, new members in leadership positions give renewed life to the Sunday School and the church.

## We Might Fail

This fear may be the most pervasive of all. The fear of failure often leads us to invoke other excuses and rationalizations for our nongrowth. We frequently want to assign the blame to our circumstances, our location, and our leadership, and so forth. We must accept the responsibility for reaching our community and quit making excuses. The church-growth principles found in Sunday School will work when they are faithfully and enthusiastically applied. They must, however, be energized by a compassion for the lost.

## We'll Lose Our Comfort

This excuse is rarely given in such a direct manner, but it is behind a host of other blinders.

"We don't have the money." Translation: we may have to give more.

"We don't have the space." Translation: we may have to build.

"We don't have the leadership." Translation: I may have to work.

"We like things the way they are." Translation: we're afraid of change.

"We don't have any prospects." Translation: we don't like visitors; we're happy with what we have.

Edd Shotwell wrote: "Believe it or not, every member of the church does not want the church to grow numerically. The status quo is just right for them. It fits them comfortably and gives them a secure feeling of position."[14] Max Caldwell echoed this concern: "Many departments, classes, and individuals in our Sunday School have been so comfortable with their circumstances that they feel no sense of urgency to reach others for Bible study and ultimately, for Christ."[15]

I can understand this natural aversion to change and a desire for comfort. With all else around us changing so quickly we look to our church for a sense of stability. Yet we cannot allow our comfort to dampen our desire to see the lost persons in our community come to know Christ as Savior. The only thing that can defeat this sort of complacency is a thorough understanding of God's purpose for the church. It was not founded to make us comfortable but to fulfill the Great Commission.

## We'll Have to Work

I once was sharing the story of our church's growth at a conference held on the Southeastern Seminary campus. After telling our growth story I fielded numerous questions about the effort required to grow a church. After the conference a pastor, who was a friend from seminary, came up to me. I'll never forget his comment. "Your talk produced two very different feelings. I want to see people saved and walking the aisles. I want to be a part of a church like that, but I'm not sure I'm willing to work that hard." At least he was honest.

The truth is that reaching the lost and growing a great Sunday School will require time, effort, and money. It will sometimes be inconvenient and uncomfortable. It will mean neighborhood surveys, evangelism training, and visiting in homes. It will entail leadership recruitment and training. It will demand excellent record keeping. It will require patience and spiritual maturity.

Are you willing to pay the price for reaching the lost? Jesus asked His own disciples similar questions before they followed Him. Leaving father and mother and selling all one's possessions were a steep price to pay. He warned them that He had nowhere to lay His head. Not very comfortable living conditions! Taking up the cross and following Christ is expensive in any generation. But the results and the rewards more than compensate for the costs. "Well done, good and faithful slave;" enter now into My rest (Matt. 25:21).

The growth of First Baptist has been exciting and demanding. We have been in a constant state of construction. Recently, we built an addition around our entire church. The whole of the building was under construction at one time, and we were still meeting in it each Sunday. It was inconvenient. There were many winter Sundays when our folks had to wade through mud to get into the building. We would lay down boards and plywood to help, but they were of little value. For much of the summer a good portion of our building was without air conditioning. It was expensive, and it was hard work. It has created some budget difficulties. Recently, we started 70 new teaching units on one day. It required an immense amount of recruiting and training of leaders to be prepared for that day. It has required a tremendous amount of work on the part of our staff and our people. Our church now meets in four different Sunday Schools—that's not comfortable for all. Our singles have been off campus for two years—that's not comfortable. But it's worth it!

## We're Not into Sheep Stealing

When I hear this, I am given the distinct impression that the speaker believes that growing Sunday Schools do so only at the expense of other local churches. First, we would all be quick to condemn the intentional raiding of other congregations as a growth methodology. It is not only unethical, but it is unproductive when we focus on the task of the church and the Great Commission. I suspect, however, that the reports of sheep stealing are often exaggerated and are used to excuse apathy and unconcern. There are, in fact, hundreds and perhaps thousands of inactive Christians in every neighborhood. The church that comes alive and begins to grow through an active program will attract some of these sheep that are running wild in the streets. Bringing neglected sheep back into the fold is not sheep stealing. Our concern must be for the kingdom of God and individuals.

It is also likely that an active ministry will attract some persons from other churches. I have heard people say "that well-fed sheep can't be stolen." This is often true, but not always. Sometimes well-fed sheep get angry or hurt and act out in an immature fashion. In their acting out, they may jump the fence in spite of our best efforts to keep them in. Some exchanging of members seems inevitable, particularly when the choices are becoming so abundant. Here we must work together to provide the nurture and care necessary to bring all of God's sheep to maturity. I'd rather know that when one of my sheep has jumped the fence or slipped out the proverbial "back door," he or she is being nurtured in a growing church than running wild in the streets.

## Notes

1. R. Wayne Jones, *Overcoming Barriers to Sunday School Growth* (Nashville: Broadman Press, 1987).

2. C. Peter Wagner, *Your Church Can Be Healthy* (Nashville: Abingdon Press, 1979).

3. Delos Miles, *Church Growth: A Mighty River* (Nashville: Broadman Press, 1981), 107-123.

4. Kennedy Smartt, "Evangelism Through Sunday School," *Pastor-Evangelist*, ed. Roger S. Greenway (Phillipsburg, N.J.: Presbyterian and Reformed Publishing Co., 1987) 116-117.

5. Ron Jensen and Jim Stevens, *Dynamics of Church Growth* (Grand Rapids, Mich.: Baker Book House, 1981), 57-59.

6. C. Peter Wagner, *Leading Your Church to Growth* (Ventura, Calif.: Regal Books, 1984), 65.

7. Kenneth S. Hemphill, *The Official Rulebook for the New Church Game* (Nashville: Broadman Press, April 1990).

8. Arthur Flake, *Building a Standard Sunday School* (Nashville: The Sunday School Board of the Southern Baptist Convention, 1922), 28.

9. J. N. Barnette, *A Church Using Sunday School* (Nashville: The Sunday School Board of the Southern Baptist Convention, 1937), 27-28.

10. P. E. Burroughs, *How to Win to Christ* (Nashville: The Sunday School Board of the Southern Baptist Convention, 1934), 15.

11. A. V. Washburn, *Outreach for the Unreached* (Nashville: Convention Press, 1960), 137.

12. Phillip Keller, *A Shepherd Looks at Psalm 23* (Grand Rapids: Zondervan, 1970), 60.

13. J. N. Barnette, *A Church Using Its Sunday School*, 31-32.

14. Ralph M. Smith and Bob Edd Shotwell, *Helping Churches Grow* (Nashville: Broadman Press, 1986), 37.

15. Max L. Caldwell, *A Guide to Standard Sunday School Work* (Nashville: Convention Press, 1982), 24.

# 4
# Sunday School and the Church Growth Movement

What do Sunday School work and the teaching of the church growth movement have in common? I have had a growing interest in this question for several years. I have read and profited greatly from a wide range of books from the church-growth field. I have also attended numerous Sunday School conferences and read the relevant Sunday School books. I found it fascinating that many of the principles, while going under different labels, were very similar.

My interest was accelerated in the fall of 1987 while I was preparing to teach a January course entitled "Building an Evangelistic Church" at Southern Seminary. I had determined to have the students read materials from the Southern Baptist perspective and from the broader evangelical field of literature. One of the books I used in preparation was Delos Miles's *Church Growth: A Mighty River*. Miles confirmed some of my feelings and spurred my interest in this comparative study. Miles wrote: "The church growth movement is in some ways analogous to the Sunday School movement."[1] Miles further stated: "It is precisely at this point of Sunday School growth that Southern Baptists may now make their most worthy contribution to the whole church.[2] Miles quoted W. Charles Arn, writing in an introduction to a special issue of *Church Growth: America* dedicated to the Sunday School and church growth, as saying: "This is a special and, I believe very important issue. . . . It is breaking ground in an entirely new area of church growth. As you will see . . . , one of the most neglected areas of applied growth thinking in the local church has been the Sunday School."[3] Arn based his observation that church-growth thinking had not been applied through the Sunday School on the fact that Sunday School attendance had declined by nearly one fourth in the last ten years.

I would contend that sound church-growth principles have clearly been taught in the writings of my denomination, but, unfortunately, they are being widely ignored not only by the broader evangelical community, but by our own constituency. Somehow the vision for growth and evangelism, the possibility thinking of our fathers has been lost in many contemporary Sunday Schools. I believe that the Sunday School provides the finest integrated growth tool on the market today. I would add one caveat to that assertion. The Sunday School functions as a growth tool only when it is energized by the focus on evangelism.

This chapter was born from the conviction that by combining an evangelistic Sunday School with an exciting worship service we have everything necessary to grow a church. Many of the church-growth principles being taught today reaffirm the historic Sunday School principles that have long been cherished by my denomination. This should not be taken in any sense as derogatory toward the church-growth movement. I am for anyone who is teaching church growth through biblical principles and reaching the lost for Christ. We are all in agreement that true church-growth principles have their origin in Scripture; therefore, it should not be surprising that generation after generation we return to a few timeless principles.

Max Caldwell was given the task in 1982 of writing *A Guide to Standard Sunday School Work*. In the preface to that book Caldwell mentioned the contributions of those who had written before him, particularly Arthur Flake. He confessed: "In researching the writing of these and other Southern Baptist Sunday School leaders, I have been impressed with the fact that while circumstances and social patterns have changed during the past sixty years, there are many Sunday School principles that are timeless."[4]

Those familiar with church-growth principles can hear the similarities by a simple listing of chapter titles in A. V. Washburn's book *Outreach for the Unreached*, published in 1960.

(1) Churches in the Midst of the Multitudes
(2) A Church Evaluating Its Sunday School
(3) A Church Discovering and Providing for the People
(4) A Church Enlisting and Developing Sunday School Workers
(5) A Church Breaking Through the Space Barrier
(6) A Church Using Goals for Developing Sunday School Work
(7) A Church Getting Better Bible Teaching Done
(8) A Church Going to the People
(9) MORE is the Word[5]

Max Caldwell in *A Guide to Standard Sunday School Work* listed nine actions that will make Sunday School a growing, life-changing organization.

(1) *Make a commitment to growth.*—Leaders and members of the Sunday School must have a commitment to growth. They must be willing to pray, study, set goals, evaluate, and report on their work. They must have a vision of what can be accomplished through the work of the Sunday School.

(2) *Identify and enroll prospects.*

(3) *Start new classes and departments.*—Beginning new units is a key principle of growth.

(4) *Enlist workers.*—Proper enlistment of workers is significant in the growth of any Sunday School. It is important that as many church members as possible be involved in places of leadership in the Sunday School program.

(5) *Train workers.*—Sunday School leaders must determine training needs, plan for these needs, conduct training programs on every age level, and recognize the leaders who complete the training programs.

(6) *Provide space and equipment.*—To keep a Sunday

School alive and growing, attention must be given to space and equipment needs.

(7) *Conduct Weekly Worker's meetings.*—Regular planning must take place if Bible study is to be effective.

(8) *Conduct weekly visitation.*—New people will not come to your Sunday School automatically.

(9) *Teach the Bible to win the lost and develop the saved.*[6]

If we are to compare church-growth techniques and Sunday School methodology, we must identify the church-growth principles. John Vaughn did a study of church-growth material and suggested there are 146 growth principles that have been proposed by various authors.[7] That finding was published in 1981. Who would hazard a guess concerning today's figure? Relax. I will refrain from discussing or listing all 146.

Delos Miles, in his excellent discussion of the church-growth principles, distinguished between principles and methods. Methods are more numerous and more apt to change than principles. Methods are more tied to a particular setting and time, whereas principles are timeless and universal. Finally, Dr. Miles has done us a great service by isolating the primary church-growth principles. These are the foundational principles that are mentioned over and over. For the sake of the present comparison I will use the list and descriptions provided by Delos Miles.[8]

## The Process Principle

Simply stated, church growth is a process and not an event. Church growth may use events, but no one or two events will sustain growth.

There are obvious implications of this principle. A process requires day-to-day, annual, and long-range planning. It requires management of time, programs, personnel, and materials, the process involves the setting of objectives and goals that can be measured and calculated. Because it is a process, it is not a passing fad. It is not a program that can be picked up and then laid aside.

The parallels in thought between this principle and the work of Sunday School are so obvious that they hardly need to be mentioned. Sunday School by its very nature is a process and not an event. J. N. Barnett, for example, talked about the value of lifelong contacts through the Sunday School.[9] Every basic Sunday School book devotes at least one chapter to the critical nature of weekly planning meetings. There is also an emphasis on monthly planning meetings and an annual preparation week. A growing Sunday School is built on effective short- and long-range planning. No one has written more extensively on goal setting than Southern Baptist Sunday School leaders. A. V. Washburn, for example, has an excellent chapter on goal setting. He wrote: "Goals are important to progress. They help us get somewhere. They help us accomplish what ought to be done." He taught that the goals must be large and visionary. Washburn insisted that goals must be measurable, accurate records must be kept, and regular evaluations made.[10]

## The Pyramid Principle

For a church to grow it must expand its base of organization and ministry before it can add new persons. To enlarge a pyramid we must enlarge its base. Thus growth means more than numbers, it means expanded administration to care for the people. This is another way of saying that we must have growth in quality and quantity.

In 1922 Arthur Flake wrote: "It will be necessary to enlarge the organization in order to take care of all the people on the church roll and those discovered in the census. There will be no use to go on with the same old organization hoping to increase the size of the Sunday School permanently. Unless the present Sunday School organization is enlarged, practically all of the work done in taking the census will come to naught."[11]

A visible representation of the pyramid principle has been provided by Andy Anderson. The "Growth Spiral" is a pictorial representation of the basic laws of Sunday School growth.

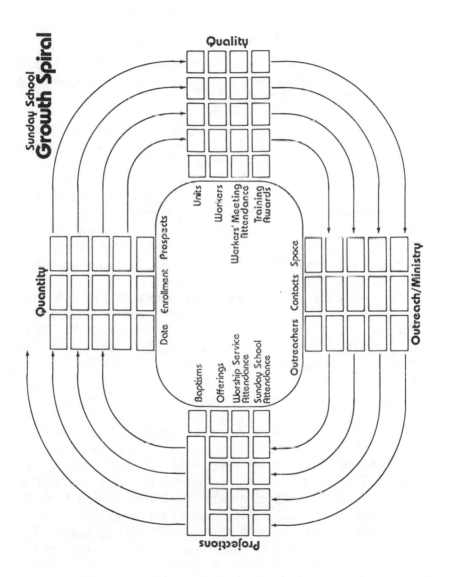

Sunday School
**Growth Spiral**

Quality

Quantity

Outreach/Ministry

Projections

Date  Enrollment  Prospects  Units  Workers  Workers' Meeting Attendance  Training Awards

Baptisms  Offerings  Worship Service Attendance  Sunday School Attendance  Outreachers  Contacts  Space

Notice that the Growth Spiral demands that we balance quantity and quality. If your church is not presently on the Growth Spiral, why do you tarry, dear Brother?

## The Receptivity Principle

Priority should be given to those who are most receptive to the gospel. We must invest the majority of our resources where they will return the most in terms of harvest. Thus church growth presents us with a number-one priority: evangelism. This principle does not suggest that we ignore those who resist the gospel. It simply places a higher priority on reaping the fields that are ripe for the harvest. Church-growth people encourage the church to be sensitive to the receptive times in the lives of individuals. To assist the church in applying the receptivity principle, some growth specialists have developed tools to help the Christian community understand the process whereby a person moves from the stage of complete unawareness of the gospel to the point where they are receptive to Christ.

I have already established in chapter 2 of this book that evangelism has long been the top priority and focus of Sunday School in my denomination. I am afraid that we lost sight of this truth for a period. I am greatly encouraged by clear signs that we are recapturing that vision once again. Perhaps we are indebted to the church-growth people for challenging us once again to prioritize evangelism. In discussing evangelism through the Sunday School, Flake, Washburn, and others employ the receptivity principle, although they do not use that term. They frequently refer to those who are enrolled in Sunday School as being most "susceptible" (Flake's term) to the gospel. They speak of reaching out to those who are on the fringe or in the contact web of the Sunday School. A. V. Washburn gave detailed instructions for reaching people who have been made receptive to the gospel by changes in life. He listed persons who are moving, those recently having babies, and persons who are shut-in or away from home. One example will demonstrate A. V. Washburn's treatment of the receptivity principle. In speaking of the Cradle Roll Department he wrote: "It has ripe opportunity for spiritual ministry at times when hearts have been softened and made aware of need."[12]

## New-Unit Principle

The growth of the church comes from new units, new members, new churches, new Sunday Schools, and so forth. Growth itself comes on new growth. Chaney and Lewis have made much of this principle. They talked in detail about new units, new leadership, new churches, and new space.[13]

This principle will warm the heart of any minister of education. I suppose if I learned anything from my exposure to religious-education classes in seminary, it was the principle of new units. Max Caldwell wrote: "Beginning new units is a key principle of growth."[14] W. Alvis Strickland wrote: "There is something about new birth that causes people to know and feel the presence of growth. New departments and classes tend to respond to this growth and environment. New units grow faster and, hence, reach more people than older established units."[15] Concerning new space, Sunday School writers are in complete accord with Chaney and Lewis. Flake wrote: "Again let it be said that a large Sunday School cannot be built and maintained in small, cramped quarters."[16] A. V. Washburn saw two keys in terms of space. "First, it is impossible to reach more people than the building can hold. Second, it is impossible to keep the attendance up to the maximum capacity of the building all the time."[17]

## The Homogenous Principle

This principle is aimed at recognizing a fact of life: people will go to church where they feel at home. The homogenous principle says that we must recognize and respect this sociological principle. A homogenous unit is defined as "a group of people who all have some characteristic in common and feel that they 'belong.'"[18] These characteristics may be education, wealth, employment, or ethnic background. This principle recognizes that the witness of the gospel travels with greater receptivity through a kinship or friendship unit. On the positive side, the homogenous-unit principle assists in understanding friendship evangelism. The homogenous-unit principle looks at each homogenous unit as a bridge for the church to move into the world. Furthermore, it assists people with identity and belonging. It emphasizes winning the family to Christ.

On balance, most church-growth writers acknowledge that this principle could be sub-Christian if it fosters a spirit of racism or elitism. It must be applied, they assert, with a sense of biblical balance. It can never be an excuse for ignoring the Christian community's role in remedying social injustices.

Certain aspects of the homogenous principle are certainly at work in the Sunday School. Strict class grading in Sunday Schools is akin to the homogeneous-unit principle. Flake wrote: "As pupils of the same age have generally the same spiritual needs, it is readily apparent that the true basis for grading in the Sunday School is the pupil's age." Flake also noted that "grading in the Sunday School creates a condition whereby people can be reached in large numbers for the school."[19] A. V. Washburn, in his chapter entitled "MORE is the Word," talked about reaching people by providing for their special needs. He followed that with an emphasis on reaching the entire family. "Have you considered your young people and provided for them in keeping with their needs? There are classifications of young people that require special provision if they are to be reached—the seventeen-year-olds, the older single young people, the married young people, the young people in college centers, and those who are away in military service. . . . If the other members of the family are to be reached adults are they key."[20] Positive aspects of the homogenous principle are present in the evangelistic Sunday School.

## Leadership Principle

The master key of the church-growth movement is leadership. A church must have the right kind of leaders and the right amount of leaders in order to grow. Church-growth writers describe the characteristics of effective pastors and lay-leaders. A few of the characteristics are as follows:

A church-growth leader—

- Must be a growing person;
- Must know the fundamentals of church growth;
- Must have a positive life-style;
- Must look to the future;
- Must set priorities;
- Must be willing to take higher risks;
- Must have a high pain threshold.

Who can recall reading a Sunday School book or periodical that did not include a special section on enlisting and training the right kind of leader? J. N. Barnett argued: "The primary problem of a pastor and superintendent in building a Sunday School is to secure and keep an *adequate number* of the right kind of officers and teachers" (my italics).[21] Flake argued that no task in the church required greater faith and more wisdom than selecting the right kind of leaders. "They should carefully go over the church roll, name by name, and make a list of all members possessing teaching gifts and qualities of leadership."[22] Flake insisted that leaders be trained in Sunday School principles before they were allowed to teach and as they continued in the job. "It is imperative that a Sunday School have a trained and intelligent corps of workers if it is to realize fully its responsibility of reaching the scores of unenlisted people in every community."[23]

A. V. Washburn listed seven requirements for leaders:

- Commitment to Christ must be without reservation.
- Loyalty in church membership must be unquestioned.
- Faith to accept responsibilities is in demand. The Lord's work needs the *right* leaders who, fully conscious of the implications, still have faith to accept the responsibilities.
- Ability to make decisions must be cultivated. Decisions and complete commitments are hard to make. Often they require unusual insight, unusual fortitude, and unusual courage to follow through. Right decisions are not always popular.

• Aims must be concentrated.

• Determination to get along with people must be sustained.

• Faithfulness to the heavenly vision must be maintained.[24]

## Small Items of Comparison

I have also found it intriguing that there are many details where comparisons can be drawn. Church-growth leaders lean heavily toward vision, enthusiasm, and possibility thinking. J. N. Barnette began his book, *A Church Using its Sunday School* with a chapter entitled "The Possibilities of a Sunday School in the Work of the Church."[25] One can hardly find a greater example of vision and enthusiasm. One could say the same for A. V. Washburn's chapter: "MORE is the Word."[26] Both the Sunday School and church-growth writers prioritize evangelism and are unapologetic about an emphasis on numbers. Many of the Sunday School writers discuss the Scripture passages concerning numerical growth that have become familiar to us through the church growth movement. Their exegesis and emphasis are quite similar. Both underline the critical need for small groups in the outreach and nurturing phases of church growth.

I found it particularly helpful to compare the ratios for church growth that Win Arn developed with the basic Sunday School philosophy.

• *Friendship Ratio*—1:7—Each new convert should be able to identify at least seven friends in the church within the first six months. Sunday School proponents have long emphasized the necessity of friendships in the small-group context of Sunday School as it relates to shutting the back door of the church.

• *Role/Task Ratio*—60:100—There should be at least 60 roles and tasks available for every 100 members in the church. While I have never encountered any ratios mentioned, I have been impressed with the recognition that the closely age-graded Sunday School provides numerous opportunities to work. J. N. Barnette wrote: "It is impossible to provide in the Sunday School a place of attractive, worthwhile service for the majority of the church members."[27]

• *Group Ratio*—7:100—There should be at least 7 groups in a church for every 100 members. If you will divide the 100 by 7 you will find that the size of the group should be around 14. Does that number ring any bells? The adult Sunday School class should have about 25 enrolled members which will allow for an average attendance of about 13.[28]

• *New Group Ratio*—1:5—Of the groups that now exist in a church, one of every five should have been started in the past two years. This ratio emphasizes once again the principle that new groups grow more quickly. We looked at this earlier. I would interject one other interesting reflection at this point. The Sunday School emphasis on yearly promotion would en able every church to meet and exceed this new group ratio.

• *Board Ratio*—1:5—One of every five board members should have joined the church within the last two years. New board and committee members bring vitality. A. V. Washburn's chapter "A Church Enlisting and Developing Sunday School Workers" lays great emphasis on seeking out and training and involving new workers. In that same chapter he gave an interesting ratio of his own. Washburn suggested that we can reach ten people for every one leader. If the church desires to grow, the ratio should be one to six.[29]

• *Staff Ratio*—1:150—A church should have one full-time staff member for every 150 persons in worship. While this is not particularly addressed by Sunday School writers, I have added it for sake of completeness.

• *Visitor Ratio*— 3:10—Of the first-time visitors who live in the church's ministry area, three of every ten should be actively involved within a year. Sunday School writers deal frequently with the follow-up of visitors through the Sunday School.

• *"Great Commission" Ratio*—3:5—At least three of every five elected officers should have a "Great Commission" conscience. Anyone reading early Sunday School authors will quickly recognize that the Great Commission was seen as the marching order of the church. They expected all those who led in the Sunday School to be "Great Commission" thinkers.[30]

## Conclusions

I am in hearty agreement with Delos Miles's suggestion that Sunday School should be seen as a major tributary in the church-growth river.

> A case might be made for singling out the Sunday School movement as a major tributary toward the church-growth river. Especially would this be the case with those denominations which have tenaciously insisted that the Sunday School ought to be an outreach and evangelistic agency of the church. The historical and traditional approach of the Southern Baptist Sunday School Board toward religious education institutionalizes and incarnates that insistence. Therefore, all Sunday Schools geared toward evangelism and missions are doing church growth, albeit under a different nomenclature.[31]

Could we be so bold as to suggest that Sunday School principles may well be the wellspring of church-growth principles? We must, in any case, learn from the writings of those in both fields.

I have, in the past several years, talked with a number of pastors and layleaders who want their church to grow. They are at a loss in knowing where to begin. Many pastors have attended numerous church-growth conferences, either sponsored by a particular church of by growth specialists. Frequently, they seem to be grasping for a particular idea or gimmick that will get them off dead center.

In the basic Sunday School organization, we have the finest single growth tool available. It is not simply one organization in your church, but the church organized for ministry.

Pastors get several good ideas and attempt to implement them in a piecemeal fashion. One program gets going, and in the meantime another program falls off. I've been there, and I understand the feeling and the frustration. You feel like the juggler in the circus who is spinning plates on the top of a stick. He gets one spinning and adds a second. By the time he adds the third plate the first plate is wobbling, and he has to go back and spin it once more lest the plate fall off and break. We have been able to overcome this problem by organizing for growth through the Sunday School. Inreach, outreach, and discipleship can be brought in under the umbrella of the Sunday School. It is the finest integrated church tool on the market today. It is not simply one organization in your church but the church organized for ministry.

One word of caution! Sunday School is only a growth tool when it is unashamedly evangelistic. Without the focus on evangelism it is simply an organization. When the Sunday School focuses on fellowship it will become introverted and will ultimately decline. Most often it does not achieve its goal of fellowship because true biblical fellowship is never introverted. The Sunday School that focuses primarily on quality Bible teaching will become cerebral and academic in nature. The Sunday School that focuses on evangelism will not only reach people for Christ but will also create opportunities for biblical fellowship and quality Bible teaching (1 John 1:1-4). You can have all three if you will *focus on evangelism* through the Sunday School. With the focus on evangelism, Sunday School becomes a living, growing organism. Evangelism is the life-giving soul of the Sunday School. We must therefore *use* it and *infuse* it. Learn and practice the principles. Infuse your Sunday School with life by giving priority to evangelism.

### Notes

1. Delos Miles, *Church Growth: A Mighty River* (Nashville: Broadman Press, 1981), 47-49.
2. Ibid., 45.
3. Ibid., 44.
4. Max Caldwell, *A Guide to Standard Sunday School Work* (Nashville: Convention Press, 1982), 5-6.
5. A. V. Washburn, *Outreach for the Unreached* (Nashville: Convention Press, 1960).

6. Max Caldwell, *A Guide to Standard Sunday School Work* (Nashville: Convention Press, 1982), 14-15.

7. Elmer L. Towns, John N. Vaughn, and David J. Seifert, *The Complete Book of Church Growth* (Wheaton, Ill.: Tyndale House Publishers, 1981).

8. Delos Miles, *Church Growth: A Mighty River,* 83-106.

9. J. N. Barnette, *A Church Using Its Sunday School* (Nashville, The Sunday School Board of the Southern Baptist Convention, 1937), 82.

10. A. V. Washburn, *Outreach for the Unreached* (Nashville: Convention Press, 1960), 91-105.

11. Arthur Flake, *Building a Standard Sunday School* (Nashville: The Sunday School of the Southern Baptist Convention, 1937), 35.

12. A. V. Washburn, *Outreach for the Unreached* (Nashville: Convention Press, 1960), 129.

13. Charles L. Chaney and Ron S. Lewis, *Design For Church Growth* (Nashville: Broadman Press, 1977), 31, 61-63.

14. Caldwell, *A Guide to Standard Sunday School Work,* 14.

15. W. Alvis Strickland, "Start New Classes and Departments," *Growing and Winning Through the Sunday School* (Nashville: Convention Press, 1960), 51.

16. Flake, *Building a Standard Sunday School,* 39.

17. Washburn, *Outreach for the Unreached,* 74.

18. David A. McGavran and Winfield C. Arn, *Ten Steps for Church Growth* (New York: Harper and Row Publishers, 1977), 129.

19. Flake, *Building a Standard Sunday School,* 50-51.

20. A. V. Washburn, *Outreach for the Unreached,* 140.

21. J. N. Barnette, *A Church Using Its Sunday School,* 36.

22. Flake, *Building a Standard Sunday School,* 36.

23. Ibid., 129.

24. A. V. Washburn, *Outreach for the Unreached,* 60-61.

25. J. N. Barnette, *A Church Using its Sunday School,* 13-24.

26. Wayne Jones, *Overcoming Barriers to Sunday School Growth,* Nashville: Broadman Press, 1987, 109-111.

27. J. N. Barnette, *A Church Using its Sunday School,* 80.

28. Jones, 109-111.

29. A. V. Washburn, *Outreach for the Unreached,* 51-71.

30. Donald A. McGavran and Winfield Arn, *Ten Steps for Church Growth.*

31. Delos Miles, *Church Growth: A Mighty River,* 24.

# 5
# Creating a Climate
# for Evangelism

When it comes to growing plants, my dad doesn't have a green thumb, he has ten green fingers. Anything he sticks into the ground grows and usually flowers or bears fruit. I, on the other hand, have never demonstrated any aptitude for the growing of plants. Nevertheless, a few years ago I was walking through the mall when I saw a display of bonsai trees. Anyone who saw *The Karate Kid* movie developed an affection for bonsai trees. I had a little time on my hands while I waited as my family looked through the various shops in the mall. The gentleman selling the bonsai trees assured me that anyone could grow a bonsai. He said that they need virtually no attention and with a little patience you would have a living masterpiece. Well, I bought it: the "line" and the tree. I took the tree to my office since I didn't want to be embarrassed in front of my family when it died.

To my amazement and delight my tree lived through the summer, fall, and winter. All I did was to water it and feed it on a regular basis. The next spring I began to notice that my tree didn't look too healthy. It wasn't long until it bit the dust. I blamed this untimely death on my secretary who had obviously not cared for the tree when I had been away. That year for my birthday my secretary bought me a new bonsai, no doubt to replace the one she so mercilessly killed.

This time I decided to spend a few minutes reading the pamphlet accompanying my tree. If all else fails, read the instructions. The pamphlet instructed me to water and feed the tree regularly. I knew that! I continued to read, thinking I had nothing to learn. "The bonsai tree you have selected is a real tree, and, therefore, it must experience the normal climatic changes of its natural habitat." I had ignored one small detail with my first tree. During that first winter, I had not provided the proper *climate* for the tree to have its natural dormancy period. I discovered a fact of life: the right climate is essential for healthy growth.

In like manner we must provide the proper climate for growth through the Sunday School. Evangelism must become a priority if we are going to experience continual growth, if we are going to fulfill the Great Commission through our Sunday Schools.

## A Description of the Environment

You may be wondering what sort of environment must be created for the Sunday School to grow and bear evangelistic fruit. There could be many suggestions, but I would like to focus on seven essential environmental concerns.

• There must be a warm evangelistic atmosphere about the church. The members of the church, the leaders of the Sunday School, and the church staff must believe in the priority of evangelism. It must be a natural part of church conversation as well as its planning.

• There must be a persuasive spirit of love. The members must actively love one another. This love must be expressed toward the community at large as a deep concern for the lost. The church must have a compassion for souls.

• There must be a spirit of excitement and expectancy. People need to be excited about what Christ is doing in their lives and in their church. This excitement leads to a real sense of expectancy. The people expect God's Spirit to move in every service. They come anticipating decisions.

• There must be a sense of urgency. When one understands the full weight of the responsibility to share the gospel and the fate of the unsaved, it will produce a sense of urgency.

• There must be an awareness of the supernatural at work.

The people must know that what is happening through them is accomplished by the supernatural power of God Himself. This comes through prayer and a dependence on the Holy Spirit.

• There must be a team spirit. Every member is integral to the growth of the church. All must be led to accept responsibility for the Great Commission, and all must experience the joy of the results.

• There must be a shared vision. Wh re there is no vision, the people perish. The vision must be communicated and shared if it is to add to the growth climate.

## Creating the Climate

How do we get there? Where do I start? We must first acknowledge that this sort of climate is not something we develop once and then simply ignore. Every member must work to ensure that the proper climatic conditions continue to prevail in the Sunday Schools and in the church as a whole. There are many forces working against this climate in the church. Forces like apathy, jealousy, lack of love, sin, and so forth. Satan will do everything in his power to disrupt and destroy the climatic conditions that are conducive to growth.

### Step One—Drop Defense Mechanism

We simply must quit making excuses for our lack of growth and our meager evangelistic results. Our biggest problem is not the church across town that is getting all the prospects. Our problem is not our community, our building, our people, our pastor, or any one of hundreds of other excuses we might want to list. Our greatest problem is that we continue to make excuses for not growing. Confess that you have been making excuses, accept God's forgiveness, and get to work.

Donald McGavran confirmed this point: "Examining the evidence, I came to believe that a major factor in the slow growth of the church was a massive buildup of defensive thinking and rationalizations."[1]

For the pastor, this means that you must accept your responsibility to lead the church in evangelism. Every Sunday School book that I have read has underlined one truth: the pastor is the key to the growth of the Sunday School. He is the head of the Sunday School in all the organizational charts, and he must become the head in practice. C. B. Hogue called the pastor the pacesetter.[2] C. Peter Wagner acknowledged that every rule has its exceptions. Some, he said, have fewer exceptions than others. One of those with few exceptions is that the pastor must want the church to grow and be willing to pay the price.[3]

Ralph Smith, a pastor of a church with a great Sunday School, states that the Sunday School must be on the pastor's mind all the time. He cannot default in his responsibility to lead the key organization in the church.[4]

For laypersons, it means that you have to want your Sunday School to grow. Drop all the selfish attitudes against growth and all the excuses that have led you to think *It can't work here.* Quit blaming others and get enthusiastically involved in the work of your church.

### Step Two—Learn the Church-Growth Principles

To make it work you need to know how it is supposed to work. My bonsai grew much better after I took the time to read the directions. Find out how the Sunday School is designed to work. If you don't presently know how to share your faith, find someone to train you. Read books on Sunday School work and church growth. When you see another church growing, find out what they are doing right. We are all in this together.

### Step Three—Dream It; Preach It; Practice It

The pastor has a great opportunity to influence the church by the very nature of his work. Dream a great dream for the Lord! Set your goals high! Expect the supernatural power of God to empower you and your church! After you have God's vision for your church, step into the pulpit and proclaim it with boldness, clarity, and excitement. If anyone needs to have a bullish attitude about the church it should be the pastor. A master of motivation is John Bisagno. He insists that the leader must be excited himself to excite the people. "They have to be revved up, plugged in, turned on, or they won't do anything."[5] The pastor has the rare privilege of communicating this dream several times weekly.

It is not enough, however, to dream and preach, you must practice what you believe. C. B. Hogue wrote that the pastor's dream must be reflected in his commitment, in his thinking, his teaching, and all his actions.[6] If you want to preach with integrity that soul-winning is a priority, you must be a soul-winner. Get involved and lead your people in visitation. If you believe that Sunday School is the key organization for church growth, then become a leader in the Sunday School.

Laypeople have many opportunities to dream, share, and practice their vision for the church. Whether you're a teacher, department head, or deacon, you must share your dream for Sunday School growth. As a department head, your teachers will go only as far as you challenge and lead them to go.

### Step Four—Focus on Soul-winning

I have already declared my conviction that evangelism is the soul of the Sunday School. Furthermore I believe that most born-again believers want to be soul-winners. Why then do so few Christians ever share their faith? Why do so few enroll in evangelism-training classes? I believe that the missing element is compassion for those who are lost. If you want evangelism to be the focus of your ministry or your church's ministry, you must first come to grips with what it means to be lost. If we ignore the eternal destiny of the unsaved, we will never be motivated to witness. D. L. Moody once said, "I see every person as though he had a huge "L" in the midst of his forehead. I consider him lost until I know he is saved."[7]

God used my six-year-old daughter to help me focus on the plight of the unsaved. I was helping her to memorize John 3:16. On this particular evening she finally quoted the entire

verse without a mistake. She was thrilled with her accom-
plishment. We hugged and kissed, then I tucked her in bed
and heard her prayers. Just as I was getting ready to leave the
room she sat up and said, "Do not perish, Daddy, do not perish." I thought, *That's cute.* But then I wondered, *Why did she
repeat those words?* I had read that verse hundreds of times
and had underlined words like "God so loved," "He gave," and
"eternal life." But I had never really focused on the phrase
"should not perish." I'm quite sure she didn't understand the
impact of those words, but the Holy Spirit used that six-year-
old to bring conviction in my life about the condition of the
lost. As I was walking back to my bedroom those words rico-
cheted around in my head. *Do not perish! Do not perish!* I real-
ized that I was doing a lot of tasks in my ministry, many of
them important. Yet I was neglecting the greatest task. If people in my community are perishing without Christ, then the
priority of my work has already been established. It is an awe-
some truth to realize that those without Christ are perishing.
They will spend eternity in hell. If you love people, a clear
understanding of this truth will motivate you to witness.

**Step Five—Practice Body Life**

A child's physical growth may be severely stunted if he or
she is unhealthy. Likewise churches must have good body life
if they are going to sustain evangelistic growth. The human
body needs balance. We require proper nutrition, exercise,
and rest. The healthy church must be well fed on the Word of
God. Members must be led to understand that service is the
proper exercise of the Christian life and a natural conse-
quence of salvation. Believers must be taught how to have
consistent quiet times in which personal prayer, meditation,
and Bible study are a regular facet of daily living. A church
must have growing Christians if it desires to be a growing
church.

Individuals, however, never grow in a vacuum. They grow
in the context of a family. The Christian grows in the context
of the church family. In Ephesians 3:17-19 Paul prayed

that you, being rooted and grounded in love, may be able to comprehend *with all the saints* what is the breadth and length and height and depth, and to know the love of Christ which surpasses knowledge, that you may be filled up to all the fulness of God (my italics).

The entire Book of Ephesians will challenge the church to become what God called it to be.

In Romans 12:9-21 there are excellent guidelines for making fellowship real in your church.[8] Encourage your congregation to minister to one another. Give them opportunities to share testimonies concerning the church's fellowship. It's good to know that the body life of your church is working. The testimonies will encourage others to be involved in the life of the body. Regular communication is vital to the growth of the body.

Healthy body life will effectively do away with the choke law. The choke law comes into effect when the existing members tend to absorb the entire time, attention, and budget of the church and pastor. God designed the church so that the members can minister to one another.

## Step Six—Equip Laypersons

One of the primary roles of the pastor/teacher, according to Ephesians 4:11-12, is "for the equipping of the saints for the work of service, to the building up of the body of Christ." If you read the remainder of that chapter you will discover the many wonderful results of the equipping of the saints. There will be unity, knowledge, maturing, doctrinal stability, honest communication, growth in every area of life and, ultimately, "the growth of the body for the building up of itself in love." This occurs only "according to the proper working of each individual part." Our people must be led to understand, appreciate, and use their spiritual gifts for the growth of the body.[9]

Train the saints and let them work. Surely the greatest untapped resource available today are excited, motivated, well-equipped laypersons. C. B. Hogue called the renewal and training of the laity the greatest challenge facing the church.

Perhaps the most important task of church growth, therefore, is the initial one of energizing—renewing—the laity. To create in the congregation's human resource pool an awareness of, and possible outlet for, the gifts God has given, is vital to the life of the church itself.[10]

### Step Seven—Organize Through the Sunday School

The Sunday School, with a heart for evangelism, is the finest comprehensive growth tool on the market today. If you have been looking for just the right tool to help your church grow, look no further. Read the classics on Sunday School organization. Go to a training conference in your state or at a denominational conference center. Go to a Growth Spiral Conference; get your church on the Growth Spiral today! The Sunday School will work! It uniquely provides the organization for outreach and inreach. *Use* it and *infuse* it with a compassion for the lost.

### Step Eight—Adopt Goals

Goals give direction and purpose to the individual and to the church. My girls and I recently purchased a small archery set to use when we are vacationing in the mountains. I was watching one day as my youngest daughter shot with no apparent pattern or results. When I asked her what she was aiming at, she replied, "What I hit." If we chose the target after we shoot, we may have marvelous short-range results, but we're not likely to grow in our archery ability.

Many Sunday Schools flounder because they have no target, no goals! Set enrollment goals, attendance goals, and baptism goals. Set a goal to have a certain percentage of your leaders trained in personal soul-winning within a year. Keep up with the results and evaluate your work. Set bold, but achievable, goals. Get some victories under your belt. Your confidence and enthusiasm will grow as people see the progress.

## Step Nine—Be Prepared to Pay the Price

Growth doesn't come without a price. While in junior high, I went through a very rapid spurt of growth. Often during this time I would wake up in the middle of the night with my joints aching, particularly my knees. When I couldn't go back to sleep, I would go to my mom for help. She would rub my knees with medicated ointment and remind me that the pain was actually a good sign. These were "growth pains" she explained. Rapid growth often produces pain. Later in high school my football coach reminded us with this slogan: "no pain—no gain."

It takes a commitment to grow. It will require hard work, money, and some inconvenience. Most of us are quite willing to pay the price in these areas. Be prepared to pay the price of criticism. Some people in the church will oppose growth. They don't want the inconvenience, the work, or the cost involved. They like things the way they are.

Hang in there! The dividends exceed the investment. The joy of seeing lost people come to know Christ, the exhilaration of seeing Christians grow in their faith, and the privilege of knowing that God's supernatural power is at work through you and your church.

## Step Ten—Bathe the Church in Prayer

Prayer is not a last step. It is rather a comprehensive and overarching one. Everything we have discussed must be done in the context of prayer. We'll never drop our defense mechanisms without prayerful confession. Evangelistic results are dependent on prayer as is the body life of the church. Good goals are discovered in concerted prayer. Prayer is the very breath of the Christian life. Prayer allows the Spirit of God to infuse and empower. Many churches have found the recent material made available through the Church Training Department entitled *Prayer Life: Walking in Fellowship with God* as an effective tool for revitalizing the church's prayer ministry.

Your church can grow! Your Sunday School will work! You can reach your community for Christ. Make a commitment right now to build an evangelistic Sunday School.

## Notes

1. Donald McGavran and Winfield C. Arn, *Ten Steps for Church Growth* (New York: Harper and Row Publishers, 1977), 2.

2. C. B. Hogue, *I Want My Church to Grow* (Nashville: Broadman Press, 1977), 66.

3. C. Peter Wagner, *Leading Your Church to Grow* (Ventura, Calif.: Regal Books, 1984), 44.

4. Ralph Smith and Bob Edd Shotwell, *Helping Churches Grow* (Nashville: Broadman Press, 1986), 26-27.

5. John R. Bisagno, *How to Build an Evangelistic Church* (Nashville: Broadman Press, 1971), 25.

6. Hogue, 77.

7. Darrell W. Robinson, *Total Church Life* (Nashville: Broadman Press, 1985), 142.

8. Kenneth S. Hemphill, *The Official Rulebook for the New Church Game* (Nashville: Broadman Press, April 1990).

9. Church Training modules, Church Training Department, Sunday School Board of the Southern Baptist Convention,

a. Kenneth S. Hemphill, *Spiritual Gifts: Empowering the New Testament Church,* (Nashville: Broadman Press, 1988).

b. R. Wayne Jones, *Using Spiritual Gifts* (Nashville: Broadman Press, 1985).

10. Hogue, 57.

# 6

# The Urgency of Evangelism Through the Sunday School

## Ways to Communicate the Urgency of Adult Evangelism

If we hope to help Sunday School members become concerned about reaching people for Christ, we must first get them to recognize facts. The world is becoming increasingly dehumanized. We live in an age where, in many people's eyes, life and its meaning have become shallow and vain. Many people are existing instead of living. They seek to find meaning in life through fruitless relationships and empty values. The fact is that many people in our world need a fresh encounter with God.

In 1987 there were 180,373,000 adults in our population—an increase of 76,529,000 (+73.7%) since 1950. By the year 1990, the number of adults is projected to be 185,231,000. Projections also indicate the number of adults to be 200,565,000 in the year 2000 and 218,394,000 by 2010. In 1987 adults comprised 73.7 percent of the total population—up 68.9 percent of 1950. Adults are projected to account for increasing proportion of the population: 74.2 percent in 1990, 74.9 percent in 2000, and 77.1 percent in 2010.[1]

The fact is: we are loosing the battle in evangelizing adults. Not only is the rapidly growing population of adults hindering our ability to reach adults for Christ, but we have also lost much of our effectiveness in reaching adults because of our apathy concerning evangelism. In 1950 it took 14 church members in my denomination to win one person to Christ. Now after several years of growth in our Sunday Schools and churches, it takes 34 members to win a person to Christ.[2]

If we are to help Sunday School and church members to become personally involved in evangelism, we must help them understand the urgency of sharing the message of good news. It is important, therefore, that we get people to understand the need for developing an effective organization in the Sunday School in order to reach people for Christ.

The first step in identifying and reaching adult prospects is to understand the definition of the word *prospect*. An adult prospect is any unsaved or unchurched adult close enough for your church to reach and minister. This person should be considered a prospect for membership.

The second most important step in reaching adults for Christ is to understand their needs. There are several ways to help members understand the need for evangelism in your community.

First, study the population trends in the community. Where are people coming from and where are they going? Your city planning commission keeps statistics about many areas of growth and development in your city. Get accurate figures related to the population of your community, the places where new housing development is being considered, and the ages of the people moving in and out of your community. As you consider the information that you gain, keep in mind that you are seeking to determine where the evangelistic prospects in your community are located. The population trends will tell you several important things regarding the need for evangelism in your community. This information will help you understand the needs in your community.

Identifying needs often gives opportunity to share the gospel. When the community is largely composed of young families, you will quickly begin to realize that if the Sunday School is to be effective in reaching people it must provide ministries to young families. The Preschool Division of your Sunday School will become an extremely important avenue of reaching young families when it is organized to reach out to young adults who are struggling to parent their children effectively.

It is at this point that many of our churches are missing

prime opportunities to evangelize because we have failed to keep pace with the increasing sophistication of the baby-boomer world and its demands for above-average experiences for their children. Young parents are no longer willing to place their preschoolers in less-than-desirable learning environments. They want the best for their preschoolers. Young parents are also increasingly demanding that their preschoolers be taught and provided opportunities for learning. Our continued emphasis on "baby-sitting" and "nurseries" at church give the impression that we are still living in the decade of the early 1950s. No longer are young parents willing to leave their children where they do not have the opportunity for a quality experience. Good or bad, the baby-boom generation is placing high expectations on their children's education whether secular or religious. These expectations, while often over enthusiastic and sometimes dangerous to the well-being of the child, are both symptoms of many of our children's problems and at the same time vivid reminders that we are living in a new world.

The fact that child care is becoming a major public and governmental concern points to the importance of providing quality learning experiences for young children in the Sunday School. When these experiences are not provided, parents are very apt to take their children elsewhere in search for such experiences. The baby-boom generation is not willing to settle for what is considered second best.

This attitude among young adults is an opportunity for the church to reach young adults through ministry to their preschoolers and younger children. Providing day care and weekday early education gives opportunity for discovering unsaved young adults who, when reached, will provide the greatest reservoir of future leadership that the church has ever known.

The key to the church and Sunday School's ability to reach these young adults will be the ability of present church leadership to begin to understand how these young adults think. When we begin to understand the way today's young adults think, we will begin to understand their needs and where the Sunday School and church can meet those needs. How many adults in your community are of the young-adult age? What is your Sunday School and church doing to reach young adults and their families for Christ. What would you have to do as a church to begin an effective ministry of evangelism with young adults? Is the quality of your ministry with preschoolers such that the young adults of your community will be challenged to become a part of the ministry your church has to offer to young families? These and other questions must be answered as part of your discovery of your communities population characteristics and trends.

Second, study the economic trends in your community. The economy of your community is a significant motivating factor in whether your community is growing or declining. Often we tend to think that there is only opportunity for evangelism when the community itself is growing. In most cases growing churches are in growing communities. However, there are exciting opportunities for evangelism in areas where the population and economy are declining. It is often in the midst of economic tragedy that people look beyond themselves for help. Unfortunately, for some people it takes a crisis beyond their resources to help them understand that they need help beyond themselves. It is often in this type of atmosphere that people turn to God for help. Our understanding of our communities' economic conditions and our sensitivity to the needs of people during tough economic times is a primary opportunity for evangelism and growth in the Sunday School. Creating groups to care for people and minister to people during these times often provides a rich climate for evangelism.

Third, study your congregation's attitude towards the facts you have discovered. What is your congregation's attitude toward the lost. Is it superficial concern? Is it apathy? Is it antagonistic? Or is it a genuine commitment to make a positive evangelistic impact on the community. This, more than any other part of the fact-finding process, and what you do with what you learn about your congregation, will affect your ability to lead your Sunday School to become evangelistic.

There is little doubt that many churches are not evangelistic because the members of the Sunday School and church are not just apathetic towards new potential members but are outright fearful and antagonistic towards those people. Why? The answer is relatively simple. Church members often become apathetic towards growth and antagonistic towards potential members because of their fear of change and their fear that they will loose their sense of importance to the congregation. It is tragic but true that many church members are more concerned about their status in the congregation than they are about people who need Jesus Christ.

These attitudes develop slowly and often over a long period of time, and are quite often as deeply ingrained in some staff members as they are in laypersons. Such attitudes begin out of a very natural desire to be a servant but can quickly lead to a subconscious need for self-esteem. Every human being has certain needs. Abraham Maslow long ago helped us to understand that beyond the physical and security needs, we all have the desire to feel accepted and needed. When we accept Christ as our personal Savior, we naturally begin to desire to serve Him. This desire is both healthy and positive. We often begin serving in what might be considered a low-profile-type ministry. Perhaps as an usher, a secretary in a Sunday School class and so forth. As we begin to serve and use the spiritual gifts that God has given to us, there is a desire to do what we do well. If we succeed in doing well, our work is often noticed by others. Perhaps someone says: "You did a great job." Up to this point everything you did is healthy and positive. You seek to do more and more because you want to serve God.

The more you do, the more you are affirmed until without realizing it you begin doing things more for the affirmation than for the service to others. If not kept in check your concern for attention, authority, and the opportunity to be a mover and a shaker in the congregation becomes more important than your service. It is at this point that it becomes important for you to preserve your roles within the congregation. In fact, in a short period of time you might spend more time preserving your role and relationship to the congregation than you do serving in the roles to which you have been called. The more you become concerned about preserving your role, the more you begin to resent attempts by others to encourage you to look into other areas of service. Almost unconsciously, you begin to act in such a manner that people begin to realize that you are really more concerned about building your own kingdom than God's kingdom.

In situations like these, some individuals link up with other individuals in the congregation who have similar concerns, and individuals become groups that block access to new members who want to become involved in the ministry of the church. These growing power structures can have a devastating effect on Sunday School and church growth. So much time and energy is spent on preserving little "kingdoms" that there is little or no time for evangelism.

Many churches across America are struggling and dying because a handful of people have become more concerned with building their kingdoms than God's kingdom. It is tragic but true that many of us are much more concerned about prestige than about the lost persons in our community.

So what can be done to turn things around and get us back to the priority of reaching people? The answer to that question is to organize your Sunday School. The process of organizing your Sunday School for growth is a prime opportunity to create new groupings of people who can have a positive impact on the growth of your Sunday School and church. These new groups begin as new units in the Sunday School and the process of organizing your Sunday School for growth and evangelism must begin with the adults.

## Adults Lead the Way

One of the primary reasons that Sunday Schools do not grow is the lack of emphasis upon adult Sunday School work. There are still many persons who see the Sunday School as a children's program. This attitude has subtly created the idea that evangelism is for children as well. There are two great difficulties with this concept. First, commitment to Christ is primarily an adult act. Second, it neglects the necessity of adult evangelization.

## The Need for Adult Evangelization

Our world is quickly becoming an adult world. This means that there must be an increasing emphasis on adult education and evangelization. We must change our attitudes toward adults and the myths that we perceive about adults when it comes to reaching adults for Christ. Here are some of the more common myths about adults and evangelism.

### Myth #1: Adults Are Not Interested in Spiritual Things

This myth seeks to make us believe that adults do not question their need for spiritual sustenance. If this were true, many adults would be much happier in life than they appear to be. The reason many adults are not happy is that they do realize there is a more effective way to live than the way they are living. Many, if not most, adults also know that God is the answer to a more abundant life. But adults are confused. They look for the answers to their questions in the wrong places. This is why there has been such religious pluralism developing in our nation in the past twenty-five years. In the past, the difference between religious groups in the United States were the differences between the Christian beliefs in the mainline Protestant denominations. Now there is an increasing plurality of ideas and beliefs between Christianity, the Eastern Religions, and the pseudo-religious groups that attempt to proselytize from the mainline denominations.

The truth is: many adults are interested in their own spiritual well-being. They are searching for answers, but they are finding a mixture of ideas, beliefs, and lack of integrity in the Christian community a formidable barrier to finding answers to life's difficult issues.

When the church seeks to make everyone conform to specific forms of religious expression and cannot both biblically and logically support the reasons for such forms of expression, the church sets itself up for failure with adults. Adults in this century want to know the *why* as much as the *how to*. Unless the church is willing to enter into an open discussion of the real life issues confronting today's adults, and does so with humility instead of a condemning view of those outside the church, our ability to reach adults for Christ will be severely limited.

The key to dealing with this myth is helping the adult members of the Sunday School and church to become aware of the needs of adults and sensitive to the opportunities to witness to adults. There are several positive things we can do to help adults to be sensitive and aware of the needs of unsaved adults.

*1. There is a need in adult evangelism to teach adults how to approach other adults concerning their religious experiences.*—There have been enough bad approaches attempted in the past that, if we are to reach adults in the present, we must learn how to share the gospel with adults in nonthreatening ways. This requires an ongoing evangelism and discipleship program which emphasizes how to talk with a person about life as well as Christ. If Christ is life, then talking about life will ultimately lead us to talk about Christ.

*2. Many adults have built a wall between them and anything that makes them think about spiritual issues in their lives.*—This may seem contrary to the prior idea that adults are interested in their own spiritual well-being. Adults do have a desire for wholeness in their lives, but they fail to understand their desires. Sound confusing? Think of it this way. Often persons with a great need and desire to be loved are so overwhelmed by the need that instead of doing something about the need they attempt to ignore it. They act as if it isn't really a need in their lives. The same is true of adults who need Christ. They do not want to admit to themselves and certainly not to anyone else that they have spiritual needs. The only way to effectively witness to these kinds of adults is through friendship evangelism. In essence, with these individuals we must become their friends if they are ever going to be able to break down the walls they have created between themselves and God. We can make a positive impact in the lives of these individuals by becoming their friends. The motivation in becoming a friend must be genuine. We cannot manipulate people into becoming Christians. We must love them enough that they realize they can trust us to talk about their spiritual needs.

3. *Our availability during the crises of life enables us to evangelize adults.*—We often have the attitude that if we cannot reach every adult let's not reach any of them. We often feel rejected if we do not succeed at reaching every person we attempt to reach. This attitude often keeps us from seizing the opportune times in the life of the adult who needs Christ. Adults who know they need spiritual direction but are unwilling or unable to do anything about the need in their lives will ultimately be confronted with crises. Crises have a way of shaking us to our foundations and making us question why we exist. These crises provide the opportunity for ministry which often opens the door to evangelism. This is why it is so important for the Sunday School to be organized for ministry. To be organized for ministry is in many ways to be organized for evangelism.

4. *Be genuine in your approach.*—Whatever method is used in meeting the needs of adults there must be genuine concern for the person involved. Adults are sensitive to the genuineness of the person who is seeking to minister to them, and they can tell when they are really cared for and when someone is doing something from less-than-worthy motives. There must be a genuine love for people if evangelism is to be effective.

5. *Invest yourself in the lives of the adults you are trying to reach.*—Evangelism requires a significant investment of yourself in the life of another person. It requires commitment, time, energy, love, and sacrifice. This may be the major reason why some Christians do not witness. It requires too much

work. It takes time to evangelize, and many of us are not willing to take the time or make the commitment to witness. If we are to make a significant impact in the lives of unsaved adults, we must be willing to sacrifice some good things in order to do the best thing.

As evangelism was defined in chapter 2, true evangelism requires discipleship. If we lead a person to Christ we should also lead the person to be a disciple. This follow-up is very important in the ability of the new Christian to grow up into Christ and become a mature Christian.

6. *We must present a positive image of the Christian life and life-style.*—This means that we must be positive about the Christian life. Many persons act as if Christianity is a burden to be endured instead of a life to be lived at its best. The rules and regulations that we require ourselves and others to observe must be biblical and not cultural. In other words, we cannot expect people to be excited about the Christian life and share Christ with others when we place nonbiblical restrictions on their life-style. The Bible is God's gift to guide us in living life at its best. When we seek to make up our own set of rules and regulations for governing the Christian life that are cultural instead of biblical, we set up barriers for the persons who need Christ. When we give nonbiblical strategies for dealing with life's difficult issues, and we manipulate the biblical text to say what we want it to say about life, we make it more difficult for non-Christians to accept the gospel. They sense that there is a difference between what we are saying and what the Bible has said or not said about that particular issue. We confuse non-Christians when we use nonbiblical responses to life.

7. *There must be a specific way of learning about the needs of adults.*—The most specific and effective way for this to occur is through the Sunday School group or care leader. These persons have the responsibility of staying in touch with every person assigned to them for ministry and outreach. Every week these persons should call every person assigned to their group and give them an opportunity to share their needs.

This type of contact reveals the real concern of the Sunday School and church for its members and prospects. If we want to make a significant impact in adult evangelism, we must get to know the prospects and their needs. The awareness of need opens the door for the presentation of the gospel in an authentic manner.

### Myth #2: Adults Are Not Interested in the Church

Our actions speak louder than our words is an often-quoted and true statement. It is certainly true in our assumptions about people and the church. We act as if every non-Christian adult has a deep hate and resistance toward the church. The fact is that most non-Christian adults do not hate the church: they just ignore it. Why? Because we as Christians often ignore it. Even when we attend church regularly we seem to ignore its teachings and impact in our lives. There are some positive things we can do to influence adults toward Christ and overcome the myth that adults are not interested in the church.

*1. We can develop friendships with people and invite them to church.*—In the USA, Lyle Schaller's twenty-five years of research shows two thirds to three quarters of all new church members responded to the church and Christ because of someone in their kinship or friendship network. In faster-growing churches the range is two thirds to seven eighths, and very rapidly growing churches these two factors (especially friendship) account for over 90 percent of the new members.[3]

This means that adults are looking for people who are excited about their church and believe that their church has answers for living life in today's world. When we fail to be positive about the church, we are teaching the nonsaved adult to ignore it.

*2. We can help adults understand that the church is not a perfect place and that it is intended to be shaped by non-perfect individuals.*—"That church down there is full of hypocrites" is a statement that we often hear. Many times the church has responded to this criticism by saying: "We are not hypocrites. You just don't understand us because you are of the world." A better response would be: "You are right. We are hypocrites. We are not perfect. We are like the hypocrites in any other organization in the world except for one very important thing. We are hypocrites who have accepted Jesus Christ as our Savior and Lord and therefore been forgiven for our hypocrisy and pointed toward becoming less hypocritical every day that we give Him full control of our lives."

The earthly church is not a place for people who are perfect. It is a place where those who are imperfect realize that they are imperfect. Then they throw themselves on the mercy of God for His forgiveness and strength. In this sense the church is a positive place because it is a place where we recognize our sinfulness and seek to become more like Jesus Christ who was perfect.

3. *Adults are looking for answers to life's difficult issues. There is a search going on in our world.*—Many adults search for stability, for a foundation that is strong enough to build a life on. They are looking for the meaning and purpose of life. Some have searched for meaning in money, status, and success only to find that these alone cannot satisfy the longings of their hearts. Many adults are searching for God. This search should end in our Sunday Schools and churches. Yet, there seems to be a reluctance by the church to share with adults in adult ways. We are more inclined in the church to treat adults like children when they are looking for an adult transformation and faith.

If we want to significantly impact adults for Christ, we must be willing to deal with some of the difficult issues we face in our world in a less than simplistic way. Too often the church seeks to answer life issues with a that's-the-way-it-is-like-it-or-lump-it attitude. When adults want to know the whys and hows of life, the church seems to think that a doctrinal statement will suffice. In order to really meet the needs of adults, there must be discussion of how the doctrine was arrived at, what it means today, and how it is to be practically lived out in the twentieth-century world.

Questions that adults are asking about life are not simplistic, so simplistic answers will not settle their longing for understanding. Our attitude might be, if they had more faith they would understand. However, it is possible that many adults cannot have faith until they understand that God loves them, and He has a plan for their lives, that there is purpose and meaning in life through a personal relationship with God through Christ.

Adults are interested in the church, but they are interested in a church which has the integrity to deal with the real issues of living in the twentieth century and not in a rehearsal of the simplistic answers to difficult problems about how to live life.

## Myth #3: Adults Are Reached by Pastors and Ministers

One of the greatest barriers to adult evangelism is that most people believe that pastors and other ministers of the church are expected to reach adults for Christ. To be sure pastors and other ministers seek to evangelize but by far most adults are reached for Christ by adults who have had no formal training in either theology or evangelism.

The gospel is still basically communicated by average persons who have experienced the love of Christ in their own lives. If we are to make a significant impact in adult evangelization, then we must help the adults of our churches to understand that pastors and ministers are not hired to do their evangelism for them. Pastors and ministers are to equip the members for evangelism and ministry.

In the past twenty years, the church has become more and more performance and spectator oriented. The church performs, and the spectators view the performance. Since the pastors and ministers are the leaders of the church they are expected to perform. When the church fails to grow and/or membership stagnates, it is because the pastors and ministers have failed to perform properly. The pastors and ministers can preach, teach, minister, and equip the congregation to reach people, but if the church fails to meet the expectations of the congregation, then all eyes turn to the pastors and ministers.

The church member often has greater opportunity to reach adults for Christ than the pastors and ministers do. The church member works with unsaved adults every day. The response of the unsaved to a witness from the clergy is often: "They are paid to do that." The unsaved do not expect church members to witness to them and are somewhat shocked and pleased when they do. If adult evangelism is to increase, the members of the church must renew their commitment to become involved in reaching people instead of expecting the pastors and ministers to do it all for them.

### Myth #4: To Reach Adults, the Witness Must Have Special Training

Training adults to evangelize is necessary and gives many people the courage to share their faith when they otherwise would not. However, we must be cautious in our evangelism training not to give the impression that one must know every Scripture and be able to refute any objections to the gospel in order to witness.

Witnessing is still simple. We simply share what Christ has done in our lives and allow the Holy Spirit to do His work in another person's life. While it is good to know the Scripture and be able to validate our Christian experiences with Scripture, it is not absolutely necessary. The thing we must know is what God has accomplished in our own lives.

There are many people who fear witnessing, most often for two reasons. They do not want to make a mistake and want to be accepted. They fear that if they make a mistake, the negative response will be their fault. They fear that if the message is not accepted, the messenger will not be accepted either.

Keeping this in mind is crucial to any real opportunity to involve large numbers of adults in evangelism. If we give the impression that great amounts of information are required to be known before one can witness effectively, we validate their fears.

We must keep before people the biblical mandate to witness and encourage members to learn how to witness effectively. At the same time we must help members understand that the greatest barrier to witnessing is their fear, not their lack of knowledge.

## Myth #5: Adults Are Evangelized Independently of the Church

Adults are independent persons and often independent thinkers. However, adults need and look for group expressions of their independence. They need relationships with other people in order to validate their own experiences. This is true in the area of evangelism as well. Adults need a community of believers with which to validate their Christian experience. Often we attempt to reach people through the masses. Perhaps the greatest motivation for mass evangelism is the lack of personal one-on-one evangelism that seems to be occurring. While this is a worthy motivation, mass evangelism often fails to help get new converts assimilated into the Christian community.

New Christians need the church the way a new baby needs a mother. Without a nurturing group of Christians to help the new Christian grow and mature, the new convert soon questions the validity of the conversion experience. This is why the Sunday School has had such a crucial role in evangelism with adults. When adults enroll in a Bible-study group, they have a built-in group of persons who can help them to grow and mature in their Christian faith.

The Christian life is not a lone-ranger experience. We need each other. As we seek to evangelize adults, therefore, we must keep in mind our relationship with God and the new convert's relationship to the body of Christ. Our evangelism program must therefore be followed up with an assimilation program if we are to fulfil the Great Commission.

## Notes

1. Clifford J. Tharp, Jr., "Adult Trends in the Next Decade," (Unpublished speech delivered to Western Baptist Religious Education Association, 24 October 1988).

2. Statistics compiled by Research Department, The Baptist Sunday School Board and reported by Harry Piland, director of Sunday School Division, The Baptist Sunday School Board.

3. Lyle Schaller, "Six Targets for Growth," *The Lutheran,* 3 September 1975.

# 7
# Organizing the Sunday School for Evangelism

Organization, who needs it? This seems to be a common question among church members. In fact, there seems to be almost hostility toward any kind of organization and planning in the life of the church. Why? Perhaps because we fear that, if we organize and plan, we may thwart the leadership of the Holy Spirit in church life.

The fear of organization can also be attributed to the fear of failure. When we organize and plan properly, we set goals; we determine a course for the future; we put our goals on paper. When we put things down on paper, accountability becomes more precise. We can tell when we reached our goals or failed to reach our goals. It just seems easier to talk about what we would like to see happen and hope that somewhere along the way we will achieve our goals. To tell the truth, it is easier to live life without accountability, but not better. In fact, life is less than fulfilling when we have determined to live it in the land of mediocrity. Our fear of failure keeps us from achieving our desired results in life, and we find ourselves empty and void of real purpose and meaning in life.

In the Old Testament Moses seems to have been at a point of desperation related to organization. As he increased his involvement in judging the people of Israel, he began to experience a great deal of frustration. His organizational skills were lacking, and his frustration turned to desperation. It was at this point that Jethro helped Moses understand that organization can be used by God to achieve His purposes. Moses had to learn that organization is basically the relationships of people to other people (Ex. 18:13-27).

The same things that happen to us as individuals happens to organizations. Organization is simply getting people in the right place at the right time in order to fulfill the objectives of the group. When the individuals who make up an organization lose their enthusiasm for the organization, it is not long before the organization begins to struggle and, if not revived, will eventually die. This has happened to countless Sunday Schools. When the individuals in the Sunday School have lost their desire and understanding of the purpose of the organization, it will not be long before Sunday School begins to decline. Creating an evangelistic Sunday School organization is a fundamental step in the Sunday School's ability to fulfill the challenge of the Great Commission and as an organization. Organizing the Sunday School for evangelism begins with an adequate understanding of the tasks of the Sunday School and how these tasks influence the ability of the Sunday School to fulfill the Great Commission.

These tasks include: reaching people for Christ, teaching the Bible, leading members to witness, leading members to minister, leading members to worship, interpreting the work of the church and denomination.[1] Of these tasks the ability of the Sunday School to fulfill the tasks of witnessing is most critical. Witnessing is not just a by-product of the Sunday School: it is at the very heart of the Sunday School's ministry. Unless average adult and youth Sunday School members begin to share their faith with others, there is very little possibility that the millions of unchurched persons in the United States will be reached for Christ, Bible study, and church membership. The following diagram illustrates the Sunday School organized to evangelize and carry out the tasks of the Sunday School and thus fulfill the Great Commission.

## General Officers Leading Out in Evangelism

The general officers of the Sunday School are the pastor, other staff members, Sunday School director, outreach/

# The Sunday School Evangelism Team

Pastor
|
Staff
|
Sunday School Director
|
Other General Officers
|

## Adult Department Evangelism Team

Department Director

Department Activities Leader ———————— Department Secretary

Department Deacon/Inreach Leader———Department Outreach/Evangelism Leader

Teacher

Class Activities Leader ————————— Class Secretary

Class Deacon/Inreach Leader ————— Class Outreach/Evangelism Leader

| Care Leader | One for | Asst. Outreach/ Evangelism Leader | One for |
| Care Leader | every four | Asst. Outreach/ Evangelism Leader | every four |
| Care Leader | to five | Asst. Outreach/ Evangelism Leader | to five |
| Care Leader | members | Asst. Outreach/ Evangelism Leader | prospects |
| | | Asst. Outreach/ Evangelism Leader | |
| | | Asst. Outreach/ Evangelism Leader | |

# Youth Department Evangelism Team

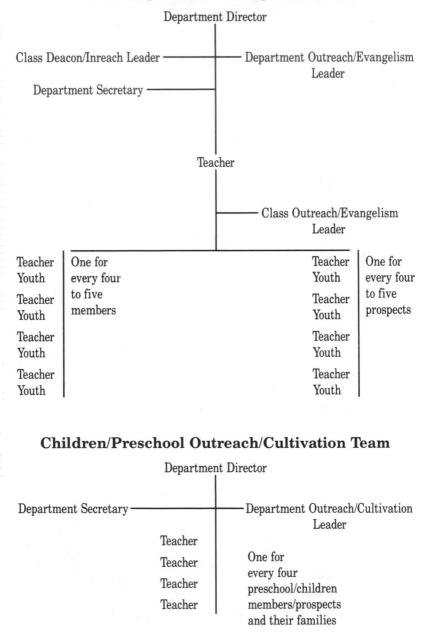

Department Director

Class Deacon/Inreach Leader —————— Department Outreach/Evangelism
Leader

Department Secretary ————

Teacher

Class Outreach/Evangelism
Leader

| Teacher Youth | One for every four to five members | | Teacher Youth | One for every four to five prospects |
|---|---|---|---|---|
| Teacher Youth | | | Teacher Youth | |
| Teacher Youth | | | Teacher Youth | |
| Teacher Youth | | | Teacher Youth | |

# Children/Preschool Outreach/Cultivation Team

Department Director

Department Secretary ——————— Department Outreach/Cultivation
Leader

Teacher
Teacher
Teacher
Teacher

One for every four preschool/children members/prospects and their families evangelism director, general Sunday School secretary, and teaching improvement director. Each of these persons plays an important role in the Sunday School's ability to become and continue to be evangelistic.

## The Pastor

The pastor's role in growing an evangelistic church could be an entire book in itself. This role cannot be fully explained in this brief section but is simply a statement of the need for the pastor to be evangelistic and lead the Sunday School to be evangelistic. The pastor is the leader among leaders in the Sunday School organization. An evangelistic pastor is one who pastors and leads the Sunday School as well as the church. If the Sunday School is the church organized to carry out the Great Commission, then the Sunday School is the pastor's opportunity to reach a lost community and lead a growing church. If the pastor is to develop an evangelistic Sunday School and church, he must do more than just preach evangelistically. He must create a climate in which the rest of the church leadership understands the importance of evangelism and sees the pastor as a model of evangelism for the Sunday School and church. He must also support the work of the Sunday School by helping the congregation understand the basic principles of Sunday School growth and how using these principles increases the opportunity to reach people for Bible study, Christ, and church membership.

## Other Staff Members

The rest of the staff have responsibility to lead specific areas of the church's ministry to be evangelistic. For example, an adult minister is responsible for leading the Adult Division of the Sunday School to be evangelistic, the youth minister is responsible for leading the Youth Division of the Sunday School to be evangelistic, the children's minister is responsible for leading the Older Children's Departments to be evangelistic and to reach the parents of children for Christ. The preschool minister is responsible for leading the parents of preschoolers to Christ.

## Other General Officers

Every general officer of the Sunday School must understand that evangelism is the key to the Sunday School's purpose and growth. General officers should be an example to other Sunday School leaders and members in the area of personal witnessing. General officers must highlight in their teaching, reaching, and leading the role of evangelism in the work of the Sunday School.

The Sunday School's ability to evangelize people and assimilate them into the body of Christ is largely dependent upon its ability to execute successfully several basic Sunday School growth principles.[2] These basics must not only be the standard by which the Sunday School evaluates its organization but also its evangelism.

## Making a Commitment to Grow

The first of these basics is making the commitment to grow. This commitment is not just a commitment to develop an organization that grows but to become an organism which evangelizes. The leaders of the Sunday School must believe that reaching people for Christ, Bible study, and church membership is of ultimate importance and make a personal commitment to do all that they can to be personally involved in reaching people and leading others to become involved in reaching people.

## Create New Units

Evangelism is strengthened by the starting of new units (departments and classes) in the Sunday School. Sunday School leaders must understand why this strategy is so important to the growth of the Sunday School and lead others to the same understanding. Evangelism and assimilation can only be effective when new units are created. The Sunday School leadership's attitude toward creating new units will impact the attitudes of the members and will greatly impact the growth or lack of growth in the Sunday School.

## Discover and Enlist Prospects

The Sunday School must continually be discovering and enlisting prospects for evangelism to occur. Specific planning must involve the members of the Sunday School in the discovering of prospects for departments and classes. Once the prospects are discovered, there must be adequate visitation and follow-up to enroll the prospects in Bible study. The enrolling of prospects in Bible study greatly increases the opportunity for evangelism to take place.

## Provide Space

The Sunday School leadership must continually be considering the best use of space for the department and classes. Once the Sunday School and worship space reaches 80 percent capacity, additional space must be provided. If space is not provided, not only will enrollment and attendance stabilize, but evangelism will also be hindered. A high priority of Sunday School leadership should be to identify the need for space before the peak of the growth in the Sunday School is diminished because enough space has not been provided. The Sunday School leadership must be alert to the trends and anticipate the enrollment, attendance, and evangelism trends of the departments and classes of the Sunday School.

## Enlist Leadership

Enlisting leadership is a continual challenge for the evangelistic Sunday School. In an evangelistic Sunday School, leaders are asked to become involved in evangelism as they fulfill their roles as Sunday School leaders. A lack of evangelistic leadership is a barrier which is difficult to overcome. Sunday School growth occurs most effectively when there are adequate leaders for the enrollment of the Sunday School, and those leaders are trained to witness to those they teach and lead.

Generally, there must be one leader for every eight persons enrolled in Sunday School for the Sunday School to be in a growth posture. The directors of departments must consistently look for potential leaders who are already evangelistic, or can be trained to be, and attempt to enlist them in the work of the Sunday School. The barrier or lack of space can be overcome, new units can be created, prospects can be located, but without adequate evangelistic leadership the Sunday School cannot grow.

A lack of new and evangelistic leadership demoralizes the existing leadership and quickly becomes a barrier to enlisting additional leaders. When workers have attempted to enlist leaders for several months and failed, they will often develop a negative attitude about Sunday School. This negative attitude then permeates the organization and creates a reticence on the part of potential leaders to become involved in Sunday School work.

There must be a continual influx of evangelistic leadership into the Sunday School organization to keep it vibrant and exciting. As these leaders reach people for Christ it challenges the rest of the leadership and membership to be evangelistic also. Department directors are catalysts for effective evangelism when they adequately affirm the workers who reach people for Christ. Sunday School leaders must know that they are encouraged to share Christ with others and that they are appreciated for their efforts in reaching people. This healthy evangelistic leadership encourages others to want to serve in the Sunday School.

**Train Leaders**

Training Sunday School leadership in evangelism is foundational in a growing Sunday School. If Sunday School work is to be conducted in excellence, we must help workers understand both the "why" and "how to" of reaching people for Christ through the Sunday School. Too often we place all of our emphasis on the how-to part of Sunday School work. We must also help members understand why we are asking them to do what we want them to do. If they do not understand why they are to reach people they will have difficulty making the commitment to reach people.

There are three basic types of training which must continually be taking place in the life of every growing Sunday School. Evangelism must be emphasized in each of these.

The first is potential leader training. Potential leader training is the type of training which gives members the opportunity to learn more about Sunday School work and decide if they would like to become a Sunday School leader. Normally, this type of training is conducted over a period of approximately eight weeks. The courses in this type of training often include: an Introduction to the Bible, a doctrinal overview, and how to teach a specific age group within the Sunday School. Potential leader training is an effective way of helping people understand the need for leadership in the Sunday School and gives the opportunity to enlist leadership who have a good idea of what they are being asked to do before they do it.

The second type of training needed for a growing Sunday School is what might be called weekly training. This type of training occurs in the weekly workers' meeting of the Sunday School. It is a time for the Sunday School leadership to plan for administering department concerns—planning for outreach, evangelism and ministry, Bible-teaching preparation, and prayer. If an effective weekly planning time is conducted for the Sunday School, there is less need for multiple training events.

Event-type training is the third kind needed in the growing Sunday School. Event training is the training that we provide at special times during the year or related to a specific emphasis in the Sunday School. Event-type training provides motivation and excitement and is needed occasionally throughout the Sunday School year. Although it is an important part of the total program of Sunday School training, it alone will not keep the Sunday School growing. If the Sunday School is to have consistent growth, there must be ongoing potential and weekly training to sustain the growth. The Adult Department director is responsible for scheduling and coordinating these types of training with the Sunday School's director of teaching improvement.

### Weekly Workers' Meetings

The weekly workers' meeting is the essential meeting of the church because this is the place where we plan for and share the results of evangelism. Most churches would not consider having a choir sing on Sunday morning without a prior rehearsal. Why then do we think evangelism will occur and life-changing Bible study take place during the week and on Sunday morning when we have not been involved in weekly planning during the week? The weekly workers' meeting is crucial in our ability to fulfill the task of evangelism through the Sunday School. Such planning must be emphasized, and attendance by leaders should be expected.

Leaders should be enlisted with expectation that they will attend weekly planning meetings and cooperate with the evangelistic plans that are made during these weekly meetings.

### Conduct Weekly Visitation/Outreach and Evangelism

There is still no substitute for meeting people eyeball to eyeball and sharing Christ with them. Yet, it is a different world than it used to be. Increasingly, it is more difficult to find people at home, and they are less willing to take the time for a personal visit. Because this is true, we must take a new look at how we think about visitation, outreach, and evangelism. We must change our ways to better express concern for people. We must be more willing to share our faith as we encounter people every day, week by week. The old adage: "If we go, they will come" is still true today. However, a more adequate statement for today would probably be: "If we go and offer people something that truly meets the needs of their lives, they will come." Prospects for the church are more sophisticated and skeptical than ever before. They want to be sure that what they need is what they get, and they will scrutinize the ministry of the Sunday School more critically than ever before. If we are to reach these people, we must make sure that our motives are pure, and the promises we make related to our Sunday School and church can be fulfilled.

### Teach the Bible Evangelistically

The Bible must be the textbook of the Sunday School, and leaders should be expected to teach the Bible for results. There are a variety of good results that occur through Bible study. The greatest result of Bible study, however, is when a person accepts Christ because of studying God's Word in Sunday School. If this is going to occur, there must be a strong emphasis throughout the Sunday School on teaching the Bible evangelistically. More will be said about this later.

When these basic principles are carried out with the purpose of reaching people for Christ, Bible study, and church membership, the Sunday School is poised for evangelistic growth.

## The Adult Department Evangelizing Adults

There are several ways in which the Adult Department adds to the ability of the Sunday School to evangelize adults.

First, the department provides the foundation for communication, and communication is essential to an effective organization for evangelism. The department period of an Adult Department provides opportunity to create a climate and motivation for evangelism and at the same time communicates the need for evangelism. The department structure also provides a better means of enlisting and developing outreach and evangelism leaders.

There must be an adequate number of outreach and evangelism leaders in place in the organization in order to reach out effectively.

Second, the department structure enables these leaders to be enlisted more effectively because it provides an added number of enlistees to the process of completing the class organization. When the department director enlists a person to be the Adult Department outreach leader, he or she is putting in place a person who will oversee and manage the outreach in the classes within that department.

If the outreach and evangelism leader does an effective job, the Adult Department director can concentrate on the weekly workers meetings, the department period, and administration of the department.

Third, the department structure gives additional accountability to the organizational structure. Not only are the leaders of the class accountable to each other, they are also accountable to the department leadership who enlisted them.

Fourth, the department structure gives opportunity for the training of additional persons who will be involved in evangelism. The department structure in Adult Sunday School involves a department director, department outreach/ evangelism leader, department activities leader, and a department secretary. In many Sunday Schools, the job responsibilities of these individuals are the same, but the name of the position changes. The key is that the Adult Department provides a structure for mobilizing laypersons in additional ways in order to evangelize adults.

Fifth, the Adult Department structure provides greater cohesiveness in the Sunday School. It is very easy for the classes of a Sunday School to soon begin to do their own thing their own way. Normally, this is not intentional. It occurs naturally when there is little communication between adult classes and their leadership. This was one of the grave concerns of the early leaders in the Sunday School movement in my denomination. If one reads the writings of Arthur Flake, J. N. Barnett, and J. M. Frost, it is easy to notice the great emphasis on the Sunday School as an essential part of the church and that each class and department within the Sunday School is a part of the church. Flake stated:

> Sunday School work is church work. Sunday school officers
> and teachers are as truly doing church work when engaged in
> discharging their duties in the Sunday School as when at-

tending the preaching service or the prayer meeting, or when giving their means to church support and missions. The Sunday School is the school of the church.[3]

The great leaders understood that if there is not cohesiveness within the Sunday School there is a tendency for unhealthy competition to develop.

The Adult Department is often the glue that holds the Sunday School together in order to keep the Sunday School moving toward common goals. The department directors are the key persons responsible for the work and management of the department which relates to the Sunday School and the classes. This person in many ways is the most important leader in Adult Sunday School work. The department director is responsible and accountable for what happens in the department in which he or she directs. If there is a problem, it is because he or she allowed the problem to occur or allows the problem to continue. If there is a victory, he or she is responsible for the management of the victory.

Too often in Adult Sunday School work, we place our emphasis on the teacher as the most important leader in the adult organization. The teacher is important in teaching the Bible effectively in the Sunday School class. The old adage "Bad teaching empties class rooms faster than good outreach leaders can fill them" is true. Without good administration of the department, however, there is normally chaos and disorganization among the classes and the goal of evangelism is all but lost.

The department director must understand the purpose of the Sunday School and be committed to the work of the Sunday School. There are ample books that describe the role and responsibilities of the Adult Department director, but because this is such an important role, insights related to this role will be expressed here in terms of the significance of the role instead of the specific responsibilities.

## The Role of the Adult Department Director as Leader

The Adult Department director is responsible to the division director in larger churches or the Sunday School director in smaller churches for carrying out the responsibilities of organizing the Adult Department to fulfil the Great Commission. For the Adult Department directors to be effective in their responsibilities as directors, they must develop the following leadership skills.

### The Director's Role As an Organizer

The director must understand the principles of Sunday School growth and the importance of organization in the Sunday School in order to be an effective leader. These principles often called the basics of Sunday School must be adhered to if the department and classes of the Sunday School are to grow.

### The Director's Role as Planner

If the department director is to be effective as a leader, the planning skills of the director must be utilized. Goals must be established, and plans for growth and improvement implemented in the life of the Sunday School. Planning involves evaluation. Evaluating where the Sunday School has been and where it is going is essential in developing plans for growth. Two essential tools for helping to determine the Sunday School's effectiveness are the Growth Spiral and the Sunday School Standard. Both of these planning tools help the director place the emphasis on the right things at the right time in order to produce growth in the lives of leaders and members.

### The Director's Role as an Educator

It has been said that "He who seeks to lead must never cease to learn." This is particularly true for the Adult Department director. The director must keep abreast of development and plans in Adult Sunday School work. This means that a regularly scheduled reading plan is a must for Adult Department directors. If the directors are going to help train, equip, and motivate the leadership in their department, fulfilling the role of educator is essential.

The director has a built-in forum for educating members in

the work of the Sunday School through the department period. These times should be used to teach members their responsibilities in adult work. Regular and periodic training opportunities should be provided for both leaders and members.

### The Director's Role as a Growth Stimulator

Department directors should be alert to new and effective ways to stimulate growth in the department and classes they lead. He or she should lead in establishing a definite and effective department outreach/evangelism program. This requires keeping the department/classes people conscious. As important as the organization is, it cannot and should not be emphasized above the needs of people. Both organization and relationships must be held in perfect balance if the Sunday School is to be considered truly effective.

Holding these two important elements in tension is difficult but rewarding. It is exciting to be a part of a Sunday School that has learned the value of balance in these two important areas of growth in the Sunday School.

### The Director's Role as an Implementer

To be an effective leader, the director must exert strong leadership that is willing to make decisions and take the blame when things go wrong. Persons who are afraid of making mistakes often fail to reach their full potential because they have not been willing to take the risk of implementing their ideas. The failure to implement what the director knows to be right is one of the most difficult aspects of serving as a leader in Sunday School. This often occurs because the director fears conflict. Conflict, however, is inevitable in Sunday School work. Effective leadership neither looks for conflict nor runs from it. Leaders realize that it is part of the task. No matter who the leader is, there will be some persons who will not like the leader's leadership style. If our fear of conflict becomes more important to us than our concern for developing an effective Sunday School organization, we will be immobilized. If we become afraid to implement ideas and principles of Sunday School growth, we will fail to achieve our potential as Sunday School leaders.

## The Director's Role as a Motivator

Motivating people to achieve excellence is one of the most difficult and rewarding aspects of Sunday School work. Every person is different, and is motivated in different ways. What is important to one may not be important to another. This is where directors must exert their leadership ability. Directors must find that common denominator that moves all of the leaders in the department to hold common values and be willing to subject their desires and wishes to the desires and wishes of the team.

The director's ability to motivate the leaders and members of the department in the area of evangelism is primarily based upon the ability to develop a trusting relationship with these persons. The only way that this trust relationship can be developed and maintained is for the director to make the process of developing relationships a priority. Evangelism is a relationship type of experience. People are often won to Christ through door-to-door evangelism. However, many of these persons never become assimilated into a local body of believers and use their gifts and abilities in service through the church. If leaders and members are going to learn how to develop positive relationships in order to reach people for Christ, they must have a model for developing healthy relationships. The director can be such a model. Through love and affirmation, leaders and members alike will find themselves wanting to become like the director and to share their love and concern with the unsaved.

## The Adult Department Evangelism Team at Work

### The Adult Department Director Leading in Evangelism

The Adult Department director is responsible to the Adult Division director in Sunday School; or, if the Sunday School does not have division directors, the Adult Department director is responsible to the Sunday School director of the Sunday School. The following are some of the reasons why Adult Department directors are so important to the work of the Sunday School.

1. *The director directs the vision of the department in harmony with the vision of the church.*—One of the essential ingredients to a dynamic and evangelistic Sunday School is the communication of the vision of the church to the grass roots of the Sunday School organization. The average and typical Sunday School member must know and understand what the church is attempting to do through its Sunday School. The director of an adult department is the primary communication link between the church and the Sunday School organization. If the director does not, cannot, or will not communicate the church's vision for the Sunday School, there is little hope that the Sunday School will accomplish its goals and objectives in reaching people for Christ.

2. *The director enlists the leadership for the organization and thus molds the department into an evangelistic team.*— The department director should have the opportunity to enlist the leadership that he or she can work with in order to accomplish the goals of the Sunday School and church. However, the department director must clearly understand the importance of such a responsibility. Handing over the enlistment of the department leadership to the director without helping the director understand the goals to be achieved is doomed for failure. There must be a real consensus of what is to be accomplished among the department leadership, or the whole process of evangelism and growth is defeated. The director must clearly be able to define the goals and objectives of the Sunday School in order to enlist the right leaders to accomplish those goals and objectives. This is an area where we often fail in our Sunday School work. We often enlist persons who cannot or will not work toward the vision of the Sunday School. Lack of leadership in the Sunday School is the main reason why. It is increasingly more difficult to enlist

committed leaders in the church. The fallout from this at times is overwhelming to those who must do the enlisting, and we end up making exceptions for those who cannot or will not commit to the things necessary to accomplish our goals and objectives.

A vicious cycle is created. We know and understand that creating new units (departments and classes) is an essential key to growing the Sunday School. At the same time, there are a limited number of persons who are willing to serve in leadership positions in the Sunday School. This creates a great tension in lives of Sunday School leaders who must do the enlisting for the new departments and classes. On the one hand there is the desire to create new units. On the other hand there are not enough committed leaders to staff the new units. What do you do? Do you create the new units with untrained and uncommitted leadership or not? This is a difficult question to answer and there is no completely satisfactory answer. The answer comes again from your vision, goals, and objectives.

Christ's command to evangelize the world is still in effect. We cannot be overwhelmed into doing nothing. The fact is: there have never been enough leaders to do the job of evangelizing the world. The early church could not get enough volunteers to help the apostles do it, and yet they did not give up. They kept enlisting additional persons in the process, and many people have been reached because of their efforts.

The same will be true of our efforts in creating an evangelistic organization for reaching adults. We will never have enough leaders to be fully effective as long as we continue to expand our organization in order to reach more persons for Christ. It is only when we settle for the status quo, when we stop creating new classes and departments, that we find enough leadership to staff the existing organization.

What is so interesting, however, is that the level of enthusiasm seems to increase when new classes and departments are being created, even when there is a great need for additional leadership. More often than not when there is a major reorganization in the Sunday School, many more workers are found and enlisted than in a year when very little changes are made. It seems that people demand something big enough to catch their interest and demand their involvement in order for them to commit to it.

In two previous instances where I have been involved in the total reorganization of the Sunday School, we enlisted more Sunday School leaders in the period of time just prior to the reorganization than in all others periods combined. In the first, we attempted to create 33 new classes and departments on one Sunday, and in the second we attempted to create 64 new classes and departments on one Sunday. In both cases we did not completely reach our goals on the first Sunday. In the first situation we created 28 new classes and departments, and in the second situation we created 70 new classes and departments. A few weeks later, we completed the organization with the additional units by enlisting additional leaders needed to staff the reorganized Sunday School. This points out the fact that potential Sunday School leaders must really know that they are needed to become involved in the work of the Sunday School.

There are many reasons for this. First, most potential leaders are very busy. They must know that what they give their time to is important. This is where we must talk with leaders about the eternal consequences of not reaching people for Christ. When we enlist leaders, we must help them understand they are becoming involved in the most important organization in the world. Their leadership as a department director, teacher, outreach leader, or care leader has eternal consequences.

Second, greater numbers of women are working. By and large, the Sunday School has had more leaders in the past because the women did most of the leading in the church. With more women working outside the home, there are fewer potential leaders than there have been in the past.

Third, potential leaders must choose between many priorities when considering a leadership position in the church today. There have been so many programs added to the ministries of most churches that the choices as to where to serve are more difficult than ever before. If the church has not adequately indicated the priorities of its ministries, many members will choose to serve in other areas that may not as effectively help the church reach its desired goals.

3. *The director can lead in the support of the church's outreach and visitation activities.*—The success or failure of the Sunday School to grow and reach its goals will largely depend upon the numbers of members in the Adult Department who have been motivated to become involved in visitation and outreach. The department director can help to motivate these persons by being an example, sharing the biblical mandate regarding evangelism, and encouraging members through personal relationships. If the director can motivate members to be involved in the church's program of outreach and evangelism, the Sunday School department and classes within that department will grow.

4. *The director can encourage open enrollment.*—Open enrollment is asking people to enroll in Sunday School the week before or on their first visit to Sunday School. Open enrollment is a proactive attitude toward reaching people. When we enroll persons before they attend or on their first visit to Sunday School, we are saying, "We want you to be a part of us, today." So often, our attitude toward enrollment has been one of merit rather than grace. Prospects often feel they must do something to be worthy of being enrolled in a class or department. An open-enrollment philosophy says: "You do not have to earn your way into membership in our Sunday School. We love and accept you the way you are. Grace has been given to us by our Lord and Savior Jesus Christ. We want you to experience His grace the way that we have experienced it."

If you were a visitor to a Sunday School, which of these attitudes would you rather be greeted with?

5. *The director can lead the department leadership team to plan for outreach and evangelism.*—One of the greatest barri-

ers to outreach and evangelism through the Sunday School is our lack of planning for it. It seems that we think that evangelism will just occur spontaneously and that it does not need to be planned. In reality evangelism through the Sunday School must be planned. Members must be trained, prospects must be secured, members must be motivated and encouraged to share their faith with others. If effective outreach and evangelism is to occur, these activities must be planned weekly. There is a need within all of us to be accountable for our good intentions. Many times we want to become involved in outreach and evangelism and will even make the first step toward involvement. But, if we do not have a plan of action and we are not held accountable for our follow-through, our good intentions become simply intentions instead of results. The department director is the primary person responsible for involving the department leadership team in weekly planning to reach people for Christ, Bible study, and church membership.

If this detailed planning does not take place in the Sunday School on a weekly basis, there is little hope that significant growth will take place in the life of the Sunday School and church. It is as the department leadership team looks at the names and needs of prospects each week, develops a daily prayer list of those persons who need to accept Christ, and plans activities to meet the needs of the prospects, that a climate for effective evangelism takes place in a department and class.

Many types of activities lead to positive results in evangelism in a department and class. Some of these include: prospect discovery, consistent prayer strategies for the unsaved, ministry to prospects, cultivation strategies for developing relationships with unsaved persons, and evangelistic training. All of these must be planned in order to be effective. As the department leadership team plans such events, it produces growth and development within the departments and classes of the Sunday School.

## The Teacher Leading in Evangelism

"The Sunday School teacher is primarily responsible for teaching the Bible to the members each Sunday" is a statement we often hear in Sunday School work. While this is true, this does not negate the importance of the teacher's influence in the lives of the members concerning evangelism. Member attitudes are often a mirror image of the attitudes of the teacher. What the teacher thinks, feels, and communicates about evangelism will have a greater impact on the lives of the members.

There are several things the teacher can do to influence the members to become involved in evangelism. The members are most closely related to their teacher.

First, the teacher can communicate the need for evangelism. The teacher must consistently be motivating the class to be involved in evangelism and modeling the way that evangelism is to take place if the class is to significantly impact its community for Christ.

Second, the teacher must be involved in weekly visitation and outreach in order to lead the class membership to be involved in visitation and outreach. The visible presence of the teacher at visitation and outreach events is essential if members are going to be involved in evangelism.

Third, the teacher must lead the class in planning outreach and evangelism events to reach the members of the class. This will require a knowledge of the spiritual condition of class members and a willingness to minister effectively to the needs of both members and prospects. On at least one week of the year, all Sunday School members who have not yet made a public profession of faith in Christ should be visited by the class leadership and members and confronted with the gospel and the need to make a public commitment of their lives to Christ. On the Sunday morning of that week, the teacher should teach evangelistically, present the plan of salvation, and give an invitation for members to respond to Christ in the Sunday School hour. The teacher should follow through with those who desire to make a commitment by going and sitting with them in worship and, if needed, go with the persons as a support when they make their decision public in the worship service.

Fourth, the teacher can create a climate for evangelism in the class by encouraging prayer. The spiritual condition of the class members should be a part of every prayer time of the class, and special prayer meetings should be scheduled to pray for the spiritual needs of the members and prospects. A praying class will be more effective in evangelism. Why? Because evangelism is basically a relational experience. When we pray for persons with whom we need to witness, we find ourselves asking for the spiritual power to effectively share the gospel with these persons. As we continue to pray, our love for these persons grows and we begin to become so concerned about them that we do not cease praying for them. Our relationships grow and before long we find that we have gained enough trust that the person we are praying for is willing to hear us as we share Jesus.

Every class ought to have a prayer list with more than just the needs of the sick. There should be a special list for those who need to become Christians, and these persons should be prayed for constantly.

Fifth, the teacher must enlist the needed leadership that enables the teacher to know the needs of members. Without constant reports concerning the needs of members, the teacher cannot teach or minister effectively to the members. Evangelism/outreach leaders and care leaders must be enlisted to stay in touch with member needs. There should be an adequate number of outreach/evangelism leaders, assistant outreach evangelism leaders, deacons, and care leaders in every class who have the responsibility to communicate with prospects and members on a weekly basis.

## Outreach/Evangelism and Inreach Must Be Balanced

For evangelism to be at its best there must be a healthy balance in the Sunday School between outreach/evangelism and inreach. Outreach/evangelism means reaching prospects for Christ and church membership. Inreach means reaching members for Bible study and ministry. If prospects who are reached through outreach and evangelism are to be assimilated into the body of Christ, effective inreach must begin immediately. If members are to be productive and fulfill their purpose as members, they must be trained and mobilized to do outreach and evangelism. A healthy balance of these two aspects of Sunday School work must be maintained in order to have a healthy and dynamic Sunday School.

The pattern of organization described here can be used to provide such a balance. This is by no means the only way to organize the Adult Department and class, but it has proven to be effective in our Sunday School.

This pattern of organization involves the deacons of the church as the inreach leaders of the Adult Division, department, and class, whose responsibility is to organize a division, department, or class for ministry to members. An outreach/evangelism leader is enlisted to organize a division, department, or class for outreach, cultivation, and evangelism to prospects.

### The Outreach/Evangelism Leader Leading in Evangelism

The outreach/evangelism leader's role in evangelism is vital to evangelizing through the Sunday School. The outreach/evangelism leader is responsible for organizing the department and class for evangelism. The outreach/evangelism leader has primary responsibility for making sure that prospects are cultivated and contacted consistently. Cultivation is especially important in creating a climate for evangelism. The outreach/evangelism leader must enlist assistants if this process is to be effective. The outreach/evangelism leader assigns to the assistants prospects, so each assistant leader has no more than five persons with which to make contact each week. The assistant then enlists members to cultivate relationships with prospects and minister to their needs.

When this process works well, it has a very positive impact on evangelism results in the class and department.

## The Deacon/Inreach Leader Leading in Evangelism

The deacons of the church can have an extremely important role in creating a climate for evangelism in the Sunday School. Deacons can serve as the inreach leader of the Sunday School class and ensure that members' needs are met. This is important to the growth of the class and department because it motivates existing members to be more involved in both class and department life and ministry and develops existing members into potential evangelizers.

The deacons' responsibility is to organize the class for ministry to members. The deacon will enlist care leaders who have the responsibility of ministering to the needs of members. The deacon assigns each care leader four to five members for ministry responsibility. The deacon's care group is composed of the care leaders. He is responsible for contacting the members of his group each week, communicating needs, sharing prayer requests, and holding the care group leaders accountable for contacting and ministering to the needs of the four to five members assigned to their care group.

As the deacon oversees this important ministry, he is fulfilling his biblical role of service and ministry through the church. As he leads in this area of work, he will know the needs of the class membership and be able to provide the spiritual resources through the membership of the class to meet the needs of the members.

## The Care Leader Leading in Evangelism

The care group leader in Adult Sunday School work has often been considered a somewhat nonessential part of the organization, almost an added frill. This is unfortunate because when the care group leaders do their jobs effectively, they strengthen the entire Sunday School. The care group leaders have the responsibility of contacting the four or five members who have been assigned to their group on a weekly basis. This weekly contact to all members gives the opportunity for the group leader to share prayer concerns, pray with members about personal needs and needs of the Sunday School and church, enlist members to attend Bible study, and enlist associate members to be involved in adult class activities. All of these responsibilities are essential to creating a climate for evangelism through the Sunday School.

As care group leaders contact members on a weekly basis, they create positive relationships with members and thus provide opportunity for the members to become more personally involved in the class or department. The care group leaders also help to reach other age groups in Sunday School by consistently staying in touch with associate members. Associate members are persons who serve in other areas of the Sunday School. These youth, children, and preschool leaders need the support and fellowship of adult members in many ways. When associate members are not given fellowship opportunities and support from the Adult Division, they often burn out and go back to their Adult Sunday School classes and departments where they can have their needs met. This sets up a vicious cycle because the Adult Division of the Sunday School must produce leadership for the rest of the Sunday School. Since we do not enlist youth, children, or preschoolers to become teachers in the Sunday School, the Adult Sunday School class must encourage members to leave the Adult Division and use their gifts in teaching the youth, children, and pre-schoolers. The care group leaders' responsibility in keeping in touch with these associate members, therefore, is important.

When care group leaders do their job effectively, they also create opportunities for evangelism. Some of the persons who have dropped out of the Sunday School and are no longer interested in attending may have never made a commitment of their lives to Christ. Through cultivation and ministry, the care group leader has the opportunity to share Christ with these persons. Through the efforts of the care leaders, members may also reach out to family members and friends. The care group leader is a significant part of the adult evangelism team and should be highlighted in the enlistment of leaders each year as the Sunday School reorganizes for growth.

## The Secretary Leading in Evangelism

The department and class secretaries are extremely important to any effective outreach and evangelism program through the Sunday School. Without clear, adequate, and correct information, evangelism and ministry are greatly impaired. The secretaries should see themselves as communicators of information necessary for the Sunday School to do its work. Each of the leaders of the adult evangelism teams must have correct information on members, absentees, and prospects. They must be able to rely on the information for correctness and timeliness.

Secretaries are much more than nickles-and-noses counters. They are a vital part of the adult evangelism team and should be part of all planning for evangelism and outreach through the department and classes.

Secretaries should be encouraged to write notes to members, absentees, and prospects on a regular basis. They should keep both leadership and members informed about consistent member enrollment, attendance, and involvement.

The Adult Department structure is one of the keys to effective evangelism through the Sunday School. It focuses the vision, commitments, and goals of the Sunday School on the parts of the organization which can most effectively help achieve these objectives. Even when there is not enough space for department periods the adult organization should be in place for the administration of department concerns, coordination through weekly workers' meetings, and motivation for evangelism.

Much information has been shared about the need for adult evangelization because there is such a great need for adult evangelism in the United States and the adult population is growing at such a rapid pace. Less information concerning youth, children, and preschool evangelism is given below, not because they are not important, but simply to emphasize adult evangelism.

## The Youth Evangelism Team

The youth evangelism team consists of department directors, teachers, department outreach/evangelism leaders, secretaries, and the youth themselves. In most cases the leaders of the youth evangelism team lead in the same way that the adult leaders do, except for the involvement of youth in evangelism. Youth are very capable evangelizers when trained to share their faith and witness. Youth should be encouraged to witness at school and to their family and friends.

Youth want to be involved in witnessing. However, they are often like adults who fear not being accepted if they let others know of their faith. Training youth in evangelism often gives them confidence to share their faith with friends.

It is good to give youth an opportunity to be involved in planning to reach other youth. They are aware of the things that will help or deter youth from coming to know Christ. Listen to their ideas, for they are much better equipped to reach other youth than adults are.

The youth Sunday School organization is the primary agent of outreach and evangelism in youth ministry. It is through inviting youth to Sunday School and getting them in a study of God's Word that they are often open to the gospel. Activities are important for youth also, but the primary place where the nurturing and training of youth can take place most effectively is through the Sunday School organization.

When the Youth Sunday School organization is functioning effectively, reaching youth for Christ is a natural result.

## The Children and Preschool Outreach and Cultivation Team

Reaching children and preschoolers for Christ happens primarily through evangelism to the parents of children and preschoolers. Children and preschool leaders have a more difficult task in reaching because the age group they lead is often not a part of the reaching process. Older children may occasionally witness, but younger children and preschoolers usually do not. The burden of responsibility, therefore, rests largely on the shoulders of the children and preschool workers. This means that the teachers must often do the contacting for both inreach and outreach.

The key to effective outreach and cultivation is understanding that children and preschool workers are building the spiritual and emotional foundations for a conversion experience in the life of the child as they teach, pray for, and nurture children. As teachers share God's love with the children and preschoolers, they develop a trust level with God that later allows them to commit their lives to Jesus Christ.

As preschool and children's workers cultivate relationships with the parents of children and preschoolers, they are creating an opportunity to reach the entire family and not just the child.

When each division of the Sunday School—adults, youth, children, and preschool—is willing to organize to reach people for Christ and make the commitment to excel in their area of the work, the Sunday School organization and its people can effectively reach, teach, minister, lead members to worship, witness, and interpret the work of the church and denomination.

### Notes

1. Harry M. Piland, *Growing and Winning Through the Sunday School* (Nashville: Broadman Press, 1981).

2. R. Wayne Jones, *Overcoming Barriers to Sunday School Growth* (Nashville: Broadman Press, 1987).

3. Arthur Flake, *Building a Standard Sunday School* (Nashville: The Sunday School Board, 1922), 17.

# 8
# Leading Sunday School Leaders and Members to Become Involved in Evangelistic Training

Before dealing with specific methods of evangelism that can be used through the Sunday School, we must first consider how to motivate Sunday School workers and members to become involved in evangelistic training.

The call to become one of Jesus' disciples is a call to prepare and train. Training is essential for Sunday School leaders and members to carry out the Great Commission. The following examples can be used to challenge Sunday School leaders and members to become involved in training.

## The Example of Jesus

Jesus was educated in Jewish tradition and religious practice. He was well versed in the Scriptures. During His ministry He quoted from at least twenty Old Testament books. Where did Jesus learn so much about the Old Testament? Primarily, His knowledge came from three sources: His home, the school associated with the synagogue, and the synagogue itself.

### His home

Jesus learned much about the Scriptures from His family. Mary and Joseph, being faithful Jewish parents, provided many opportunities for Jesus to learn about God. Scripture parchments kept over the door or tied to the wrist provided them with opportunities to share God's Word. The daily prayers, lighting of the sabbath fire and lamp, and celebration of important feasts also were part of Jesus' education.

For His birth Jesus was trained to be a good Jew, to love God and His neighbor, and what it meant to be a part of the Jewish nation. Training in each of these areas helped prepare Jesus to carry out His mission.

## The Synagogue School

Jesus also learned from the school that was a part of the synagogue of His day. The school met each weekday. Attendance was probably compulsory. A Jewish boy began school at age six and continued through age ten. He was required to study Scripture, beginning with the Book of Leviticus. From his tenth to about his fifteenth year, a young boy was trained in Jewish oral tradition.

Jesus' training was rigorous and demanding, but He studied faithfully that He might be prepared to do the work of His Father

## The Synagogue

Jesus also learned from the synagogue. It was customary, if not mandatory, for Jewish men to attend the synagogue on the sabbath. Luke stated: "as his custom was, he went into the synagogue on the sabbath day" (Luke 4:16b, KJV). In each of the synagogue services, a portion of the Torah (the first five books of the Old Testament) was read and then interpreted. A second reading was given from the Prophets. Luke recorded at least one occasion when Jesus was called on to interpret the prophetic meaning of Scripture (Luke 4:17-19).

Thus, Jesus learned from the Law and the Prophets and was able to discuss Scripture intelligently with the rabbis of His day.

## The Example of the Disciples

The twelve men whom Jesus called to be His disciples, He also trained to evangelize a lost world. These twelve men were willing and eager to learn all that they could from Jesus. From the first day they met Jesus until their last meal together in the upper room, the disciples were constantly being trained to fulfill the Great Commission. When Jesus said, "Follow Me," He was saying to the disciples: "learn from Me; take My teachings and implement them in your life."

The disciples revealed their willingness to train when they asked Jesus for help in how to pray (Luke 11:1). They were willing to follow Him throughout Jerusalem and Galilee to improve their understanding of God and how they could teach others about God.

In the upper room, Jesus spoke to His disciples about how they should live when He would no longer be with them. He said that the Holy Spirit would remind them of all things that they had learned from Him (John 16:4-14).

Even though He was the Son of God, Jesus was willing to be trained. The disciples followed His example and willingly trained to be Jesus' disciples and to do Kingdom work. If we are to reach our lost world for Christ, we must be willing to be trained in how to reach people for Christ.

Sometimes Sunday School leaders and members grumble and complain when asked to become involved in training. It is sometimes difficult to get leaders and members to understand the importance of training. Training motivated workers and members to be more effective in their jobs is essential for evangelism to occur through the Sunday School. But what if you cannot get the leaders and members to participate in training. The following suggestions may be helpful.

*1. Expect leaders and members to participate.*—Perhaps the greatest indicator as to why persons do or do not become involved in training is whether they believe it is expected that they will be involved in training. Most of the time we get exactly what we expect from leaders and members, no more and no less. When we do not expect that leaders and members will be involved in evangelistic training and witnessing, they will not become involved. If we tell them that it is difficult and hard to witness, they will expect it to be difficult and hard. But if we share with them the positive experiences of witnessing, then they will become excited about sharing their faith with others.

Every leader and member has a responsibility to witness. We cannot say that witnessing is someone else's job or that we are not gifted to do it. Indeed, we may not have the gift of evangelism, but that does not mean we have no responsibility to share what Christ has done in our lives with others.

2. *Point out the benefits of participating in evangelistic training.*—Many leaders and members do not understand the benefits that come from being involved in evangelistic training. These benefits include: enthusiasm, confidence, spiritual and emotional support, and joy.

### Enthusiasm

The word *enthusiasm* symbolizes the excitement that occurs when God is working in the lives of His people. In fact, the word *enthusiasm* comes from two Greek words *en theos,* which means "God in us." When we are enthusiastic, we are allowing God's power to work in and through our lives to influence the lives of others. When we allow God's power to move us to witness, we are enthusiastic. When we organize the departments and classes of our Sunday School for witnessing and evangelism, we are enthusiastic. Enthusiasm is more than an emotion. It is a way of life when we allow God to live in us.

As the members and leaders of the Sunday School become enthusiastic, the Sunday School begins to grow. Without enthusiasm, the Sunday School seems dull and dead. If we want to effectively fulfill the Great Commission we must allow God to empower us to evangelize.

### Confidence

Another benefit of evangelistic training is the confidence it gives to those persons who learn how to witness. For most of us, fear is the greatest barrier to evangelism. When we have the opportunity to learn and practice sharing our faith with others, we become more confident in our ability to share the good news. Evangelistic training can prepare us to witness in a variety of situations. Confidence is a must if witnessing is to become a life-style. If we are afraid we will make mistakes, our ability to witness will be extremely limited. Evangelistic training cannot ensure that we will not make mistakes, but it will give us confidence that what we are sharing is indeed biblical, personal, and meaningful.

**Spiritual and Emotional Support**

If evangelism is to be central in our lives and in the life of our Sunday School and church, we must feel that we are not alone in our desire to share Christ. Evangelistic training gives us a tangible and visible indication that there are others within the body of Christ who want to learn how to share Christ with others in the most effective way.

Through evangelistic training there is the opportunity for the development of teams which pray together, witness together, and evangelize together. As people gather together for training to better understand the nature of evangelism and how to do it, they gain both spiritual and emotional support from one another. If you can remember your childhood, you know that it is easier to do something you fear if you have a friend who is willing to do it with you. Evangelistic training helps to create the bonds, friendships, and support needed to cultivate an ongoing program of evangelism in the Sunday School.

**Joy**

Evangelism training also gives opportunities to experience the joy of sharing Christ with others. Most adequate evangelism training programs have a report-back session where those involved in witnessing can share their experiences, and the joy they find in seeing people come to know Jesus Christ as their Lord and Savior. Without these expressions of joy, evangelism loses its excitement and soon becomes a responsibility instead of an opportunity.

Joy should be shared beyond the report-back sessions of evangelistic training. If we want our Sunday Schools to really become involved in evangelism, these experiences should be shared in the Sunday School departments and classes also. When joyful experiences are shared with other Sunday School members, they motivate others to become involved in evangelism. When was the last time someone in your Sunday School departments or classes shared the joy of seeing an unsaved person come to know Christ? As the joy is shared, many will want to become involved in evangelism through the Sunday School.

## Lead by Example

For members to really catch the vision and experience the joy of evangelism, the leadership of the Sunday School must lead by example. Leaders must be the models for sharing Christ through the Sunday School. This means that there must be a real commitment on the part of Sunday School leaders to share Christ with others. Leaders must be present and lead the evangelistic and prospect visitation of the Sunday School. As members see their leaders not only talking about evangelism but also involved in it, they will begin to follow the examples of their leaders.

This is perhaps the greatest motivator for evangelism through the Sunday School. Members are encouraged and challenged when they see their leaders involved in reaching people for Christ, Bible study, and church membership. If the members hear their leaders talk about evangelism while not being involved in it, they will soon turn a deaf ear towards their leadership when it comes to growing the Sunday School. Sunday School leaders must be effective models for evangelism if evangelism is to be effective through the Sunday School.

### Affirm Those in Evangelistic Training, Visitation, and Witnessing

Everyone enjoys the feeling that comes from having been applauded by their peers. Affirmation is an important aspect of developing behavior. When we affirm those people who are involved in evangelistic training, visitation, and witnessing, we are developing positive behavior in the Christian life.

It is unfortunate that as Christians we often criticize people who need affirmation to continue in their service. We believe that they should not need affirmation in order to keep on keeping on. If all of us were already perfect and mature as Christians, it is possible that we might be able to live life without affirmation. Most of us have not yet reached that point, however, and we need to feel loved and cared for in order to do our most effective work. As we affirm those persons we see involved in evangelistic training, visitation, and witnessing, we create a climate in which others will want to be involved in evangelism.

## Training Sunday School Workers and Members in Evangelism

There are many ways that Sunday School workers can be trained to share their faith. Not every Sunday School worker will respond to the same approach. This is why in recent years there has been a proliferation of training materials for evangelistic training. It would be impossible to overview all types of evangelistic training materials available today. This overview will seek to show the variety of options available and how to motivate people to become involved in evangelistic training.

### Using a Marked New Testament

Using the Scripture as a guide for witnessing is not new. In fact, it can be traced to the New Testament church. Philip used the Book of Isaiah to share the gospel with the Ethiopian eunuch. The eunuch was saved and baptized as a result. It is one of the most effective ways to share the gospel because the message of the gospel comes from the Scriptures. God's Word promises us that it will not return void. Both the Old and New Testaments still continue to be messages of hope for the world. There are many Scriptures that can be used to share the gospel message.

## Training Sunday School Leaders to
## Share Their Personal Testimony

The Holy Spirit can use your personal experience with Christ to help other persons place their faith in Him. Simply share what your life was like before accepting Christ: how you repented of your sins; how you are allowing Christ to be Savior and Lord of your life in the present. Share how Christ changed your life and why His presence in your life makes it meaningful and abundant here and now. Do not underestimate the power of your personal testimony. Remember that the apostle Paul often used his conversion experience as a means of sharing Christ. The following may help you to prepare your personal testimony.

Many Sunday School leaders have learned a written or memorized outline of the gospel. Such an approach is practical and reliable in most witnessing encounters. Both Continuous Witness Training and Evangelism Explosion use a model presentation of the gospel as a tool for witnessing. In general, both of these presentations are based on the following: Man's Need, God's Response to Man's Need, Man's Response to God's Plan. One could very effectively use this outline of the gospel using these three headings with Scripture.

Using the basic introduction of CWT, one can quickly and effectively begin sharing Christ with evangelistic prospects. The word *FIRE* can be used to help you begin the gospel presentation. This brief outline includes sharing about family, interest, religious background, exploratory questions.

With this simple outline, any Sunday School leader should be able to adequately share the gospel with an evangelistic prospect. The key to this process is sincerity. Really be concerned about the individual you are witnessing to.

Begin the conversation talking about your family and the prospect's family. Draw comparisons between your family and the prospect's. Allow the Holy Spirit to develop a caring relationship between you and the person you are sharing with.

Next talk about the prospect's interest. What is it you and

your new friend find interesting and exciting about life? Talk about your religious background and ask the prospect about his religious background. At this point you may want to share your personal testimony and conclude by asking: "Has anything like this ever happened to you?" Lastly, ask the question: Have you ever personally placed your faith in Jesus Christ as your Lord and Savior, or are you still considering it? This will open the door for you to lead the prospect to a commitment to Christ.

Unless we as Sunday School leaders can overcome our fear of witnessing and lead the members of our Sunday Schools to witness, there is little hope that we can reach the millions of unchurched people in our communities.

## How to Share a Witnessing Pamphlet

The simplest way to use a witnessing pamphlet is to read the booklet to the person whom you are sharing with. You might begin the conversation by asking the question: If I could share a very brief statement with you that could forever radically change your life in a positive way, is there any reason why you would not let me share the information with you? This question helps you to get the attention and interest of the person with whom you are attempting to share the gospel. It is also important at the beginning of the conversation to say, "I promise that at anytime you wish to stop me you may do so, and I will honor your request." Often, people have a fear that someone will get them into a situation where they feel uncomfortable. If they know, however, that they have control of the situation and can cease the conversation at any point, they begin to relax and will likely allow you to continue.

Next, you will need to make sure that the person understands what you are sharing. It is good from time to time throughout the presentation to ask if what is being shared makes sense to the person. As you read the pamphlet, remember the information that you are sharing may be completely foreign to your listener. Focus on the needs of the person with whom you are sharing and not on your feelings. If the person with whom you are sharing stops you at any point and says he or she does not want you to continue, honor their request and ask, "May I give this pamphlet to you as a free gift?" Remember that it is the responsibility of the Holy Spirit to convict of sin, bring about repentance, and confession, and regeneration. It is your responsibility only to share.

## Training Sunday School Leaders in Evangelistic Prospect Cultivation

An effective program of evangelism through the Sunday School will be multifaceted. Just as every adult does not learn in the same way, not every Sunday School leader or member is going to feel comfortable with only one approach to evangelism. Some Sunday School leaders will never become involved in a formal program of evangelism. Some people, for whatever reasons, may be much more inclined to develop friendships with people to reach them for Christ. This type of evangelism is often called friendship evangelism or relational evangelism. Friendship or relational evangelism emphasizes the importance of cultivation in the witnessing process. Cultivation is defined as a planned approach to developing a relationship with unsaved persons to share the gospel with them.

Oscar Thompson emphasized this approach in the book *Concentric Circles of Concern*. Indeed, friendship does have a very positive impact on evangelism. In the New Testament there are many places where a person who has just become a Christian immediately goes and shares the gospel with a friend or relative. This one-on-one type of evangelism is still the most effective way to reach people for Christ because trust is an essential ingredient to faith. We often distrust people we do not know. As we become friends with other persons, we begin to open ourselves more fully to them. In the process we allow them to share with us the important aspects of their lives because we trust them.

In our day, trusting relationships seem to have become a thing of the past. There is a real reluctance in our society to trust each other. The development of relationships, therefore, becomes an important factor in our ability to evangelize our world. Cultivation is the process of planning relationships with those persons who need to hear and respond to the gospel. To effectively cultivate an evangelistic prospect, a method must be developed for keeping track of relationships created. A cultivation diary is an excellent way to record information and attempts to cultivate evangelistic prospects. The cultivation diary should be used to record every activity used to develop a relationship with the evangelistic prospects you are attempting to reach. Recording such information gives you confidence to continue to witness.

### Suggestions for Cultivating Evangelistic Prospects

1. Pray daily for prospects.
2. Enlist prayer support from your Sunday School class leaders and members.
3. Make a friendly visit to the prospects.
4. Be alert to special needs in the lives of the prospects and their families.
5. Take prospects to an acitivity that they enjoy, such as a sporting event, to cultivate friendship.
6. Invite prospects and their family to your home for dinner.
7. Send prospects special occasion cards, like a birthday card and Christmas card with a personal note.
8. Take prospect to as many Sunday School class and department activities as possible.
9. Enlist Sunday School members who are neighbors to visit the prospect.
10. Work with the Sunday School teachers in trying to enlist other members of the prospect's family.
11. Telephone the prospect and encourage him or her to attend special worship services with you.
12. Write a personal note of encouragement and enclose a witnessing pamphlet.
13. Share your personal testimony of what Christ means to you.

# My Cultivation Diary

## Information on Prospect

Name _____

Home Address _____ Phone _____

Business Address _____ Phone _____

Year of Birth _____ _____ Date Assigned _____

Spiritual Condition: _____ _____

_____

_____

## (Inside Pages)

| Date | Cultivation Activities |
|------|------------------------|
| _____ | _____ |
| | _____ |
| | _____ |
| **Date** | **Cultivation Activities** |
| _____ | _____ |
| | _____ |
| | _____ |
| **Date** | **Cultivation Activities** |
| _____ | _____ |
| | _____ |
| | _____ |

14. Use a marked New Testament to show how to be saved.
15. Try to enroll the prospect in Sunday School.
16. Seek to lead the prospect to receive Christ as Savior and Lord.
17. When the prospect accepts Christ, help him or her to grow in the Christian faith.

## Training Sunday School Leaders
## Through Continuous Witness Training

Perhaps the most exhaustive and complete witness training course ever designed is Continuous Witness Training.[1] CWT, as it is often called, is made to be used in conjunction with and as part of the overall outreach program of the Sunday School. The participants in CWT are the pastor/leader, apprentices, certified witnesses, equippers, encouragers, and prayer partners.

The pastor must attend and certify at a national CWT seminar. He serves as the equipper for at least one cycle. Apprentices are staff or laypersons who desire to learn how to witness and are willing to make a commitment to participate in 13 consecutive weeks of training in evangelistic witness and visitation.

Certified witnesses are staff or laypersons who have certified by completing the 13-week CWT cycle as apprentices in a local church. Equippers are certified witnesses who have successfully completed a 13-week cycle of equipping two apprentices. Encouragers are members of the Sunday School who are not involved in the CWT equipping process, but who are willing to make an 11-week commitment to work through the *Survival Kit for New Christians* and encourage them to attend Sunday School and worship.

Prayer partners are other church members who are not involved in the CWT training process but who are willing to pray for those who are and the prospects they visit.

During the CWT training sessions the apprentice will memorize and learn to use a "Model Presentation" of the gospel, develop skills for witnessing, and work through the following session titles:

1. The Role of the Holy Spirit in Witnessing
2. Giving Your Personal Testimony
3. Approach to Witnessing in the Home
4. God's Purpose
5. Our Need
6. God's Provision
7. Our Response
8. Leading to a Decision
9. Follow-Up
10. Dealing with Objections and Questions
11. Building Witnessing Relationships
12. Multiplying Witnesses
13. Certification

For a local congregation to begin to use CWT as an evangelistic training approach, the pastor and preferably one other leader must attend a CWT seminar and become certified. These seminars are conducted across the nation in local churches by the Personal Evangelism Department of the Home Mission Board.

For dates and locations of such seminars contact your state evangelism director or the Home Mission Board.

## Lay Evangelism School

The Lay Evangelism School is designed to teach adults and youth how to witness.[2] Training in the classroom along with on-the-job training are essential ingredients in this important type of evangelism training. The Lay Evangelism School involves 13 weeks of continued training. There are five phases of an effective Lay Evangelism School. These are the preparation phases, spiritual preparation, people search, intensive training, and continued training. In the preparation phase, the church's staff and lay leadership develop the various committees needed to conduct the school. The committees have the following responsibilities: promotion and registration, spiritual preparation, people search, material requirements, arrangements, and witness assignments.

In the spiritual-preparation phase, six weeks of study are led in the areas of The Lord, The Bible and Prayer, The Holy Spirit, Your Christian Witness, Your Christian Life, and Your Church.

Following this phase, the People Search Committee needs to locate evangelistic prospects who will be visited during on-the-job training visits. Prior to people search, the Materials Committee ensures that all needed materials are on hand for the people search and training.

The training involves nine hours of classroom time and three hours of on-the-job training. These twelve hours of intensive training usually are scheduled two hours each evening from 7:00-9:00 p.m. Monday through Friday, and Saturday or Sunday afternoon. The classroom sessions include three types of training divided into Bible study, creative activities, and witness demonstrations. Step-by-step help is given in how to witness. Following the training, actual witnessing assignments are made and visits attempted. Reports on the visits are encouraged and expected.

The total Lay Evangelism School experience consists of a three-month preparation time, one week of intensive training and three months of continued training.

In leading Sunday School leaders and members to become involved in evangelistic training, we must remember that we are leading people. Every evangelism program or training event must be designed to meet the needs of the people presenting the gospel and the needs of those who need to respond to the gospel. If we are to significantly impact the millions of lost people in our nation, we must lead them to become involved in evangelistic training.

## Notes

1. For further information about Continuous Witness Training, contact the Personal Evangelism Department, The Home Mission Board, 1350 Spring Street, NW, Atlanta, Georgia.

2. For further information about Lay Evangelism Schools, contact your state Evangelism Department.

# 9
# Teaching Teachers to Teach Evangelistically

The Sunday School is the greatest organization ever created to evangelize our nation for Christ. If Sunday School is ever to reach its potential for evangelism, however, Sunday School teachers must be trained how to teach the Bible evangelistically. The Bible is the textbook of the Sunday School. The key to its effectiveness in the lives of people is the ability of the teacher to share adequately the written and living Word. In other words, we must teach people the Bible.

## Teach People the Bible

The key to effective Bible study is the correct understanding of the purpose of the message of the Bible. The message of the Bible is to be directed toward people. We are not just teaching a book: we are teaching people The Book. For the Bible to become life changing in the lives of the people, there must be effective relationships and communication with the audience. The key to excellence in Bible teaching, therefore, is creating an atmosphere of openness and trust in which people can study, probe, and clarify their thinking about the biblical message. Too often the message is not comprehended because the person teaching does not adequately take into account some basic teaching/learning principles. What are some of these principles?

First, the relationship between the teacher and the pupil must be one of concern, trust, and friendship. Without these ingredients the teacher cannot adequately address the needs of the pupil, and the pupil cannot respond positively to the message. The teacher must find ways to communicate love and concern for those being taught. All of us have at some time in life experienced a teacher who we knew really cared about us. For those teachers we studied harder, learned more, and our desire to learn intensified. The same is true of the Bible teacher. Without concern, compassion, and friendship the teacher can teach, and the pupil can learn, but neither will ever reach their full potential in the teacher-pupil relationship until there is mutual concern, trust, and friendship.

Second, the teacher must motivate the pupil to think. It is important that Sunday School teachers teach their members to come to their own understanding of why they believe what they believe and not just accept the teacher's word. Excellent teachers teach their members to think, not just accept. They know that until the teaching becomes a reality in the life of the pupil, there is not real foundation for growth in the pupil's life.

Third, the teacher must create a healthy tension in the life of the pupil. This tension is the dynamic of which all good teaching is made. The pupil must come to the point in his life where there is tension between what he knows or suspects and what he does not understand or believe. This tension is necessary for growth to take place in the pupil's life. Normally, people do not study, grow, or mature when not confronted with a question or issue they do not understand how to deal with. It often takes a crisis to create the right atmosphere for new learning and growth in the life of the pupil. The teacher sometimes must move the pupil to question things not questioned before to help the pupil grow.

Fourth, the teacher must emphasize application of information. Have persons really learned if they do not do something with what they have learned? That is a difficult question to answer. One which is not as difficult to answer is: Should persons do something with what they have learned? Excellent Bible teaching is more than imparting facts. Excellent Bible teaching emphasizes the need to apply what has been learned in everyday experience. One of the great difficulties in effective Bible teaching is getting pupils to do something with what they have learned. In thousands of churches each Sunday, the Bible is taught. What are people doing with all they are learning in these Bible-study lessons? Are they indeed using it? Unless the teacher emphasizes application of Bible learning to everyday life, there is little quality Bible study taking place.

Fifth, there must be an opportunity to respond to the biblical message. In most Bible-study sessions a lesson is taught, members are led to a point of understanding the message, then the lesson ends. There is little opportunity to respond in this type of approach to teaching. Unless the pupil can respond to what has been communicated, the learning process is effectively shut down. To lead the pupil to understand the message and then fail to allow the pupil to respond to what has been learned is ineffective. When done consistently, this type of teaching teaches the pupil not to respond. In essence, this kind of teaching frustrates the learner into a nonreactive posture. Effective Bible teaching calls for action.

With these teaching/learning principles in mind, how do these relate to evangelistic teaching?

## Evangelistic Relationship Principles

The teacher-pupil relationship must be one of concern, trust, and friendship for evangelism to take place. The relational aspect of evangelism is at the heart of the experience. If the persons who need Christ do not feel that the person sharing Christ is concerned about their needs, it will be very difficult for the prospects to respond to the message. A climate for evangelism in a Sunday School class is a healthy climate where mutual concern, trust, and friendship takes place. For this to occur, the teacher must be concerned about being an effective evangelistic witness who makes sure that positive relationships are developing between members of the class and prospects. Once potential members feel accepted by the individual members and the class, the opportunity for evangelism increases dramatically. If the teacher is to help develop such a climate, he or she must learn relational skills as well as methodology and theology. The teacher must be able to be a friend, a good listener, an honest witness, a counselor, and a person who can accept responsibility for witnessing. In other words, the teacher must be spiritual leader and model of a Christian witness for the members of the class.

The more a teacher learns how to help members develop healthy relationships with one another and teaches concern for one another, the more likely the class is to become evangelistic. To develop such positive relationships among the class members and evangelistic prospects, the teacher and class members must:

## 1. Be a Friend

The teacher who wants to be effective as a witness must be a friend to the prospect. To have friends we must be a friend. We must take the time and energy to develop friendships. The key to making friends is to be available when our friends need us. In Jesus' ministry He always seemed to be at the right place at the right time in order to provide friendship. The woman at the well (John 4), the man born blind (John 9), and the healing of the demoniac (Mark 5) are just a few examples which point to the fact that Jesus was there when He was needed. The witness must see as a basic responsibility taking time to develop friendships with the persons he or she is seeking to reach. This is not easy. Some people do not know how to be a friend or to accept the friendship of others. From early childhood some fear having a friend because to have a friend we must make ourselves vulnerable to being hurt. Most of us know what it feels like to be let down or disappointed by our friends.

While this can bring great pain, it can also bring great joy. The teacher who wants their Sunday School class to be evangelistic must work very hard to cultivate relationships and friendships between class members and prospects.

## 2. Be a Good Listener

For people to share their real concerns about their spiritual health and well-being, they must feel that they can trust the person with whom they share their concerns. The teacher can develop this kind of relationship with the class member or prospect by attentively listening to the needs of the class members and prospects. By listening the teacher must listen for both words and the attitudes behind them. When teachers can listen to members and prospects, they have opportunity to hear about their life concerns. These life concerns provide clues to the member or prospect's relationship with God and others. These clues often lead to the opportunity to present the gospel to members and prospects. For this type of relationship the teacher must develop the art of listening to others. Every person in the class must be challenged to think about his relationship with Christ.

## 3. Be Honest

Being honest with yourself and the individual you are attempting to reach is basic in any successful attempt to present the gospel. What is your motivation for sharing Christ with this individual? Do you really want to see the person come to know Christ, or will your personal image be enhanced if you can reach someone for Christ? In other words, are you reaching out to this prospect who needs Christ for what Christ can do for him or for what *you* will get out of the experience? Your motivation for sharing Christ will greatly influence your ability to reach the person for Christ. If your motivation is something you are doing for yourself, you will soon lack the motivation to follow through with the person.

If the motivation for sharing is your own self-esteem, then you will also find the person with whom you are sharing seeking to distance herself from you. As human beings we often sense when the motivation of others to help us is really a deceptive attempt to help themselves. If the prospect feels that way, she will quickly attempt to terminate her relationship with you.

Be honest with yourself and the prospect. If you are developing a relationship with the person in order to share Christ with the individual, there is nothing wrong with that as long as you realize what you are doing and are willing to love the person even if you can't reach the person for Christ.

### 4. Be a Counselor

Being effective in evangelizing others often requires counseling by the person who is attempting to witness for Christ. Very often it will be a specific problem or difficult experience one is dealing with that moves the person to seek Christ. It is important, therefore, as you attempt to share Christ with others to develop your skills in the area of counseling. While it is important to understand some basic principles of counseling when helping people with their problems, one does not have to be a certified counselor in order to encourage those who are struggling with important decisions in their lives to place their trust in Jesus Christ. Be open to the opportunities that come your way to counsel with those who are dealing with difficult situations in their lives. Your willingness to counsel with these individuals may open the door to share Christ with them now or sometime in the future. Your ability as a teacher to counsel with your members can be a beginning point for helping them to help others come to know Christ.

### 5. Be a Person Who Can Accept Responsibility for Your Witness

This means both teacher and class members must realize that their witnessing and evangelistic responsibilities are not fulfilled until the person who has been reached has also been incorporated into the life and ministry of the class and church. The best definition of evangelism includes the assimilation of the persons who are evangelized into the body of Christ. Once the evangelistic prospect has made a commitment of life to Christ, he must also be assimilated into a group of believers who will care for him on an ongoing basis. This happens in the Sunday School as these persons are assigned to a small care group where they are constantly and consistently contacted and cared for by the members of the Sunday School class to which they belong.

## Evangelistic Teaching Principles

Evangelistic Bible teaching depends upon the evangel. Unless Christ is proclaimed, there is no opportunity for evangelistic teaching. The question that quickly comes to mind is: Can Christ be proclaimed in every Sunday School lesson? The answer is yes. The teacher can use almost any Scripture to lead members toward Christ if the Scripture is applied to the needs in the members' lives. For example, one would probably not think that the genealogy narratives in the Old Testament related to Abraham and his descendents could be used evangelistically, but if the teacher could use this Scripture to point to the importance of family and the need that every individual has to be a part of a family, one could very easily begin to point to the needs of class members and prospects to be a part of a family of faith. Since Christ is the door by which we enter the family of faith, it would then be easy to share who Christ is and how one becomes a child of God and thus a member of the family of faith.

This example merely points out that almost any Scripture can be used to move the Bible study in the Sunday School toward the evangelistic. It is important not to take Scripture out of context or distort the message in any way, but in most cases the Scripture of the Bible study can be shared in such a way as to become evangelistic in nature.

There are several evangelistic teaching principles or methods that can be used to teach evangelistically through the Sunday School. These include: praying for the power of the Holy Spirit, identifying evangelistic text, interpreting Scripture in light of Christ, praying specifically for non-Christians, teaching the basis for abundant living, modeling the Christian life, emphasizing evangelistic truths, seizing the teachable moment, and moving from the general to the specific.

## Praying for the Power of the Holy Spirit

Evangelistic teaching is powerless without prayer. The Holy Spirit can do in the lives of people what we can never do. As preparation for teaching begins, prayer must begin. Teachers must ask the Holy Spirit to bring into focus the spiritual needs in the lives of members. In our human understanding alone we cannot discern where people are hurting or how to relate the Scripture that we are preparing to teach to the specific needs of the members of our class and evangelistic prospects. We must rely on the Holy Spirit and the insights that He gives to us in order to clearly identify the true needs of the persons we teach. This does not mean that we do not do everything possible to understand human behavior and response and just rely on some sort of "magical spiritual insight." It does mean, however, that we must attempt to analyze, with the help of the Holy Spirit, the words that people say and the behavior we observe to help us understand where a person is in relationship to Christ and the Christian life.

Evangelistic prayer intercedes for other persons in order that they might hear, understand, and respond to the evangelistic message. It is prayer that moves beyond the prayer itself to actions which reveal our love and concern for those persons with whom we have the opportunity to share the gospel.

As we prepare to teach the Bible evangelistically we need to write down the name of every person whom we will be teaching and ask the Holy Spirit to lead us to identify the spiritual and evangelistic needs in their lives. One person's name may be placed on paper, and beside it the need identified may be salvation while another name may be placed on paper, and the need identified may be for that person to become an evangelistic witness. This should be a weekly event in the life of every teacher as preparation is made to teach God's Word each week. Each teacher should ask the following questions about every member or prospect: *"What is the evangelistic need in the life of this member or prospect, and how can I apply this week's Scripture to meet that evangelistic need?*

*What can I personally do besides teaching this lesson that will help this member or prospect understand the biblical and evangelistic message which they need to hear? What evangelistic actions can I take to show that I really love and care for this member or prospect?*

Praying for the power of the Holy Spirit as you prepare and as you teach will help you to teach the Bible evangelistically.

### Identifying Evangelistic Text

Another aspect of teaching evangelistically is identifying evangelistic texts. Our ability to identify effectively whether a specific text is evangelistic or not is determined by how we think about Scripture. The written revelation of God is the Bible. We interpret the Bible not only by what it says and means but also by the human revelation of God in Jesus Christ. In other words, we interpret the written Word by the life of Jesus Christ who is interpreted to us through the written Word which is the Bible. In order to think both biblically and evangelistically, we must, therefore, ask two questions as we consider the use of Scripture evangelistically. First, how does this Scripture enlighten us and help us to understand more about Christ? Second, how does the life of Christ help enlighten us and help us understand more about this Scripture? As we ask these questions, we can see that most Scripture can be used to teach evangelistically.

As we begin our preparation to teach, we must continually keep in mind that Scripture interprets Christ, and Christ interprets Scripture. When we read the background and focal passages of each week's lesson, we should look for opportunities to interpret for members and prospects how that specific Scripture interprets Christ, and how Christ interprets that Scripture.

Evangelistic lessons are sometimes highlighted, so the teacher can easily identify those lessons that are highly evangelistic in nature. This does not mean that other lessons are not evangelistic in nature, it simply means that some lessons are more easily prepared for an evangelistic response. It is wise for the teacher to go through each of the lessons in a unit of study before the lesson begins and identify those passages in the background and focal passages that can be used to emphasize the gospel message, so all of the lesson can be tied together evangelistically as well as methodologically.

### Interpret Scripture in Light of Christ

This may seem redundant, but it is important that the teacher take every opportunity to focus the Sunday School lesson on Jesus, the pivotal Person and personality of the Bible. When Sunday School lessons are Christ centered, everything taught focuses attention on Christ and every person's relationship to Him. If the Bible-study hour is focused on Christ, then it cannot be focused on other things. The time allotted for Bible study on Sunday morning is so brief that it is very easy for other things to crowd out the centrality of Christ in the Bible-study hour. In many Sunday Schools after announcements are made and the fellowship time is over, there is barely more than twenty minutes for Bible study which focuses on Christ. If we truly want to interpret Scripture in light of Christ, we must not allow other things to keep us from studying the Scripture on Sunday morning.

### Move from the General to the Specific

As you teach, move from the general application of Scripture to the specific application of Scripture. It is one thing to talk about how to become a Christian; it is quite another to help specific class members or prospects to understand how they can become Christians. Share the Scripture in such a way that the members and prospects can see that the lesson material does not just relate to people in general but specifically to them and their need for salvation. The content of the session must at some point move from the *they* and the *we* to the *you* and the *I* in order for life-changing and evangelistic Bible study to occur.

**Pray Specifically for Non-Christians to be Saved**

Not only should prayer focus our attention asking the Holy Spirit to help us as we prepare to teach the Bible evangelistically, but our prayers should also focus on the unbeliever. In praying for the unsaved we pray for the person. We pray that God's Holy Spirit might penetrate the heart and bring an awareness of sin. We pray for courage that the unsaved persons will be able to confess their sins to God. We pray that unsaved persons will ask for the forgiveness of their sins and make a commitment of their lives to Jesus Christ.

Our prayer for the unsaved must be ongoing. If a significant change is to occur in the hearts of those persons who are most resistant to the gospel, God's people must pray continually for the unsaved. The Sunday School teacher must lead the class to pray for the unsaved above all else in the life of the class. Special seasons of prayer should be planned for those who are unsaved. For this to be effective, the class must have an up-to-date list and the spiritual condition of those persons for whom they are praying. The prayers should be specific and consistent.

Besides the verbal witness, prayer is the most important ingredient in an effective evangelistic challenge to the lost persons that the Sunday School and church are attempting to reach.

**Teach the Basis for Abundant Living**

There is little doubt that most people are looking for what they consider to be "the good life." This is evident in our society as never before. There seems to be an obsession with living a life that seems to be free from difficulty and struggle. Most people believe that this type of life is available to them through wealth and material possessions. This critical desire for the good life is perhaps the greatest avenue that the Christian community has for introducing the unsaved to Jesus Christ. People are searching for the good life, and the Christian knows the reality of abundant living. It is important, therefore, for us as Christians to share with the unsaved the good news that indeed there is a "good life," and that abundant life is available to everyone through Jesus Christ. The good news is that life can have meaning and purpose. We find that meaning and purpose in our relationship with Christ.

Sharing the good news, therefore, depends upon defining for the unsaved the true nature of the good life and that it does not depend upon what one has but who one knows. This is difficult for the unsaved person because he or she is continually inundated with information which says that the only way to the good life is through wealth. If we are to effectively witness to the unsaved, we must find ways to identify the ingredients of the good life and compare those ingredients to the presentation of the good life offered by society. Society's good life is made up of money, prestige, power, influence, popularity, and fame. God's good life is made up of peace, discipline, devotion, love, and healthy relationships.

As the world seeks to hand out the good life through self-gratification, God seeks to give us the good life through self-sacrifice. Jesus said: He who would follow Me must deny himself, take up his cross and follow Me. It is in this sense that the cross is still such a scandal. We cannot accept that the good life comes from self-denial instead of self-indulgence. We must help those whom we seek to share the gospel with to see that the good life comes only from the abundant life that Jesus Christ can give to us.

### Embody the Christian Life and Its Principles

The Christian life is a life of relationship with Jesus Christ, and relationships must be embodied. The Christian life is not just a theory or grand idea. It is an experience to be lived. The greatest witness that a teacher or class member can give to the world is to embody the love, grace, forgiveness, and character of Jesus Christ. The goal of the Christian life is to become more and more like Jesus Christ everyday. Unless we are willing to live out what we say we believe about being

Christian, there will be very little impact on those we seek to reach for Christ.

In the Book of Acts, it was the model that the early Christians presented to their world which so influenced their society for Christ. In Acts 2:41 we are told that the Christians held all things in common and the Lord added daily to their number those who were being saved. This means the example that the Christians set for their society was so radically different from their world standards that the unsaved were impressed with the early Christians' commitment to their Lord and one another. These early Christians did not simply talk about their commitment. They proved their commitment everyday by the way in which they lived their lives. This same kind of embodiment of the gospel is needed today. The world is looking at the Christian church to see if it really is different and whether Christianity really does work. The greatest witness we give to our world is a daily example of God's grace to a broken world.

**Emphasize Evangelistic Truths**

It is imperative that teachers and members of the Sunday School emphasize the evangelistic truths of the Christian life. Some of these truths are: self-control brings self-fulfillment and effective living, generosity results in kindness, love overcomes evil, forgiveness frees us from being imprisoned by guilt, and relationship to God places us in a position of receiving grace.

The unsaved need to know that a relationship to Christ actually works. The evangelistic truths of the Christian life really do free us to live life at its best. The truths that God's Word gives us empowers us for effective living. A relationship with Christ does not stifle our spirit, minds, emotions, and wills but energizes us to a life of excellence instead of mediocrity, power instead of futility, and enthusiasm instead of apathy.

When Jesus said that He came to give us life abundantly, He meant that He came to give us life at its best. The natural conclusion is that unless we have life in Him, we have no life at all. We are simply fooling ourselves if we think we are living life until we allow Him to live in us.

These are the great themes that we must be emphasizing as we relate to our friends and neighbors in the daily experiences of life. These are the things they need to hear. They are looking for someone who can give them some reason for their existence, some hope for despair, and some confidence for their living.

As we teach and as we communicate concerning the nature of life and our reason for existence, we must emphasize these eternal and evangelistic truths with as many persons as possible.

### Teach for Evangelistic Response

Teaching for a response is essential if there are to be significant results from evangelistic teaching. As we share God's Word and Christ's sacrifice for us, we must plan for and expect a response. God's Word tells us that His Word will not return void or empty. We must challenge people to respond to the gospel and expect that people will respond. As we teach evangelistically in the Sunday School class, we must give members and prospects the opportunity to respond. At the end of an evangelistic teaching session it makes little sense to just close with a prayer and give members and prospects a specific way to respond to what has been taught. It may be that when concluding an evangelistic teaching session, you will want to pray the sinners' prayer and ask those who feel they need to respond to the message that has been presented to pray the prayer with you. You may want to ask members or prospects who would like to know more about how to become a Christian or who are ready to make a commitment of their lives to Christ to stay after class and talk with you about their decision. Whatever the method, there must be opportunity for persons to respond to the evangelistic message, or there is little use in sharing it.

Once persons do respond, it is important for you to provide

encouragement for them, to follow through with their commitments. When persons in the class accept Christ as their Lord and Savior, it is important to encourage them to be baptized and become members of the church. You may ask them if you can attend worship with them and walk with them when they make their commitments public before the congregation. However you do it, it is important for you as the teacher or one who has helped these persons make the commitments of their lives to Christ to make specific responses to the gospel message.

### Seize the Teachable Moment

The word *eureka* basically means "aha." It describes those moments in our lives when we experience understanding of something that we have never understood before. As we teach, guide, and lead people toward Christ, there are those teachable moments when just the right words at just the right time create a "eureka experience." We sometimes call this the teachable moment. In evangelistic teaching we must seize the teachable moments when persons are being convicted by the Holy Spirit to make a commitment of their lives to Jesus Christ. During these times we must be extremely sensitive to the leadership of the Spirit as we teach. At these moments we must lead the class in such a way that interruptions are avoided, concern is expressed, and opportunity to respond is prioritized.

In these teachable moments we must be willing to stop and answer questions, be sensitive to needs, and ignore the unimportant so that the most important can be dealt with effectively. These teachable moments may be rare, therefore, we must not miss them when they occur. These are the times when people accept Christ during the Sunday School hour. There is nothing that will excite a Sunday School class more than for members to be a part of a class where someone accepts Christ while studying God's Word.

As a teacher looks for those teachable moments and seizes the opportunity to realize the potential for an evangelistic harvest, the Bible can be taught evangelistically on a consistent basis through the Sunday School. Indeed, if life-changing Bible study is to take place in the life of the Sunday School, the Bible must be taught evangelistically every week as the class gathers for Bible study. There are literally thousands of persons who will come to Sunday School for the first time now and in the future. When they come, they will come either consciously or subconsciously to hear a word from God. When they come, they will come with the opportunity for their lives to be changed. If they come and the gospel is not presented evangelistically, and there is no or little opportunity for response, we may never get the opportunity to share with them again. What takes place on Sunday morning in Sunday Schools across our nation has eternal consequences. We must do our very best to ensure that the gospel is taught evangelistically, consistently, and effectively each and every Sunday. The training and support we offer our Sunday School leadership must, therefore, be consistent, effective, and excellent. Teaching the Bible to win the lost and develop the saved is at the heart of any effective Sunday School organization. Our Bible teaching must not become a redundant rehearsing of unincorporated experiences. It must be exciting, applicable, and authenticated in the lives of those who teach and those who learn. When Bible study becomes exciting, applicable, and authenticated in the lives of those who teach and those who are involved in it, then it is evangelistic teaching.

# 10
# Assimilating and Conserving Evangelism Results Through the Sunday School

Assimilating new converts into the body of Christ may be the most difficult part of the evangelism process. Because the Sunday School is organized not only to reach people for Christ but also to minister and keep in touch with members on a weekly basis, it is the most effective organization in the church for assuming the role of assimilation. Before the assimilation process can be clearly developed, we must understand church membership from the new Christian's perspective. When persons become new members of the church, they bring with them certain expectations that if not met will hinder the assimilation process.

First, new members need to feel important to the group. *Group* here means the class to which they belong, the staff of the church, the circle of friends in which they socialize, and the church as a whole. This is particularly true of the persons who have just received Christ as their Savior.

Try to think back to the time you were a new Christian. This is very hard for many believers because they accepted Christ when they were very young and grew up in the church. The new Christian faces at least three obstacles to becoming assimilated into the church.

### Obstacle 1: Fear

Perhaps the greatest obstacle to new Christians becoming assimilated is the fear of making a mistake that will be noticed by the group. There is an unwritten code of conduct for the new Christian which basically states that the person is a new person and no longer excused for sinful acts. The attitude of many Christians toward new Christians seems to be a "Let's wait-and-see attitude." This attitude is sometimes very judgmental, and the criteria for living up to the attitude is based on a churchly culture, not biblical teachings. The new Christians have great pressure to conduct themselves in such a way that they are seen as different than they were before their conversion experiences. To be sure, there will be changes in the life and life-style of the new Christian but to expect that the new Christian will not slip up, make mistakes, and sin is to consider the new Christian to be something other than human. New Christians sense that they are being watched and thus fear making mistakes that will be noticed. This fear is very detrimental to the growth of the new Christian for it places undue pressure on the person not to make mistakes. The idea that we cannot make mistakes keeps us from planning our growth and being willing to risk ourselves in order to grow. When we become so fearful of making mistakes or failing, we find ourselves immobilized and unable to move forward. Our fear of failure becomes a self-fulfilling prophecy.

The next great fear of the new Christian is the fear of rejection by the group. The new Christian like all of us has an enormous need to be and feel accepted. There is a great deal of difference in being accepted and feeling accepted. We often question why some people do not become assimilated into the body because it is our feeling that they were loved and accepted by the group. We must deal with not only the realities of the persons being accepted but with their perceptions as well. A person can be accepted by the group, but unless the person feels accepted the reality is rather insignificant. These fears can only be overcome with love. As the apostle John said in 1 John 4:18: "There is no fear in love. But perfect love drives out fear, because fear has to do with punishment. The man who fears is not made perfect in love" (NIV).

There are several "must" actions which must be taken by the group if it is to assimilate new members and new Christians into the group.

*1. The group must understand the urgency of making the new member and new Christian feel welcome and do everything possible to make this occur.*—Name tags are important to the group which wants to assimilate new members. Knowing the name of an individual is still extremely important in creating an atmosphere of warmth and acceptance. We want people to know our names, and who we are. Growing groups emphasize wearing name tags. Name tags are used by all members, not just new ones. One of the most unwelcome things we can do is to make the new member feel conspicuous.

We often do this when we make the new members wear name tags and do not require the existing members to do so. Another way we do this is by making the new members stand and tell something about themselves. We must remember that the new member may feel very uncomfortable being in the limelight because of shyness. Until they feel accepted by the group, new members should not be put in this position.

*2. One-on-one relationships and smaller group relationships should be fostered by the group.*—There should be one person or a small group of two to four assigned within the group to help the new member feel accepted. The emphasis here is on getting the new member to be asked to participate in events which make the new member feel a part of the group. The best way for this to occur is for the new member to be invited to the home of a classmate to whom he or she is assigned. There is something about eating together and being in the home of another individual which generates warmth and friendship. Within the first three weeks after new members join the group, they should be invited into someone's home for a time of getting to know one another and fellowship.

*3. Friendship must be established quickly.*—Getting more than the name of the new member is important in establishing lasting relationships with the group. A brief survey or questionnaire should be filled out by new members asking questions like: When is your birthday? What do you enjoy doing most? What are your hobbies? Do you have children?

What are their ages? Where do you work? What are the things you most like to do as a family? These surveys or questionnaires should be photocopied and placed in a notebook in the class and department to be used by members in getting to know one another. Remember, everyone in the group should fill out the information. A symbol unknown to the new member might be used somewhere on the information to indicate that the information is about a new member so that extra special attention can be given to that individual.

4. *Informal fellowship activities must be scheduled.*–For new members to feel welcome and accepted, they must have the opportunity to participate in informal fellowship activities. These should be scheduled regularly by the group. Again, name tags are important at those events, and there should be a combination of group and smaller group activities within the fellowship. A group activity might be a game or learning experience. The smaller group one-on-one opportunities can be either arranged or just allowed to happen spontaneously.

In these fellowship activities there should be opportunity for more than just social fellowship. True Christian fellowship occurs only when there is some degree of evangelism and in-depth Christian growth involved.

### Obstacle #2: Lack of Concern

Another of the obstacles to new members becoming assimilated into a local body of believers is our lack of concern about assimilation. Often we expect new members to find a place in the body on their own. This is like assuming that the new baby will know about nutrition and know how to feed itself. If we are to help new members become assimilated into the body, we must be willing to take the time and energy to help them find their own way. There are several things we can do to help people find their place in the body.

1. *We can provide new member orientation.*—New-member orientation gives new members the opportunity to learn

about the church in which they are becoming members. The new member should be held accountable for attending such an orientation because it is so essential to assimilation into the church. When new members are present or absent from new member training, they should be contacted each time they are absent and encouraged to attend the next session. This is a good way to help the new members understand what will happen when they are absent from Sunday School and help them feel comfortable with being contacted on a weekly basis.

2. *We can help new members discover and use their spiritual gifts.*—The New Testament teaches us that every Christian has at least one spiritual gift, and some Christians are multigifted. In 1 Corinthians 12:7 Paul said: "Now to each one the manifestation of the Spirit is given for the common good" (NIV). Sometime during the assimilation process (first three to six months), the new members should be invited and expected to attend a seminar on discovering and using spiritual gifts.

Inventories are available which actually point Christians in the direction of their giftedness, so they can begin to use their gifts, and the body of Christ can begin to confirm gifts within the membership of the body.[1]

3. *We can assign someone to new members for follow-up and friendship.*—All new members need someone whom they know they can call on when they need information or help. Some people are afraid to call the church office and ask for information. They may need someone who knows about the church and can answer their questions. Such assignments are best made related to the interest of members. For example, it is good to put parents together in such assignments because they are going to be concerned about the ministries offered by the church for their children.

### Obstacle 3: Loss of Our Influence

We often create obstacles for new members with our attitude toward our own leadership within the congregation. We may think that if we allow new members to become assimilated into the body they will take our place of leadership in the fellowship, and we will lose our influence or power within the church. This can be a subconscious or conscious concern, and it is the reason why we often place either written or unwritten stipulations on when a member can assume a job within the body. In some churches this is at least three months; in others six months; in others a year. We must understand that the longer we wait to get people involved in the life and ministry of the church, the less likely it will happen.

## Factors that Affect the Assimilation of New Members

There are several factors which affect a church's ability to assimilate new members into the body. These must be addressed to conserve the results of conversion and church growth through biological growth and transfer growth. These factors include: identification with the vision, friendship, small-group, leadership, time, accountability, and homogeneity.

### Identification with the Vision

For evangelistic results to be conserved and new members assimilated, these persons must be able to identify with the vision of the church. When potential members are looking for a place in which to confess their faith and serve their Lord through a local body of believers, they are looking for a place that gives them direction for their spiritual lives. The vision of the church as proclaimed by the pastor and the church's ability to communicate that vision is essential to the assimilation of new members into the church. This vision is something that is caught more than it is taught. When you walk into a church whose vision is clearly established in the mind of the pastor and church, it is very obvious. It is something that you begin to feel as you greet the members of the church, as you read the church's promotional and communication pieces, and as you participate in the Bible study and worship of the church. The key ingredients that create this vision are the pastor's leadership style, the style of music and worship, and the awareness on the part of the people that "this is a place where God is present."

The pastor's leadership style is so keyed to this vision that without it there is little that can be accomplished in the growth of the church and the acceptance and assimilation of new members. The pastor's style is obviously evangelistic in nature. The concerns that are expressed in the pulpit through the worship, through the announcements, through the music, through everything that occurs clearly states that the purpose of the Sunday School and church is to carry out the mandate of the Great Commission, and every member of the body of Christ has a specific responsibility to be involved in evangelism. As the pastor leads in any and every area of ministry, it is evident that the church's time, energy, and resources are prioritized towards evangelism.

A second key ingredient in the creation of a vision that people can identify with is the style of music and worship. In growing churches where the unsaved are being reached in large numbers, the worship is celebrative, open, less than formal, and praise oriented. The worship experience itself says that the staff and people are comfortable with one another, open to one another, and those who are not yet members are welcome to join the "family." The sermon is personally oriented and deals with the practical issues of life—how to obtain and live the abundant life that Jesus Christ wants to give to us. The music and worship moves people to experience the presence of God in their lives and thus leads to the third, and perhaps most important, ingredient in the creation of a vision that people can identify with.

This is the feeling among the members that their church is a place where God is present. They do not mean by this that God is not present in other churches, but they do mean when they come to church they are not surprised to experience and encounter the living God. They expect that when they come to worship God in their church that something exciting is going to happen. They expect that the music will be great, the preaching will be practical, and that people will respond in obedience to Christ.

When people can identify with this type of vision in the life of a Sunday School and church, they are challenged and impressed to join the church and become involved in the life and ministry of the church.

### Friendship

In order for new members and new converts to become assimilated into the life of the church, they must be able to develop friendships with several members in a very short period of time. People do not stay where they do not feel accepted, wanted, or needed. Every new member needs to be able to identify at least six to eight friends within the first six months after they join the church. If these friendships do not occur, the new member is almost never assimilated into the body. This friendship factor has particular significance for the Adult Sunday School classes of the church. Most friendships occur in a small-group setting; therefore, the Adult Sunday School class becomes the place where friendship is most likely to occur for the adult member. If the climate in the class is not warm, open, friendly, and nurturing, friendship will be stifled, and new members will not be assimilated.

When friendship is not encouraged and intentionally planned in the adult class, the excitement of the music and worship experience is lost. The climate of the classroom, therefore, can drive people away from the church more quickly than the music and worship experience can create excitement about potential membership. There are several elements that contribute to the ability of a class to be a place where friendships can occur. These include: the attitude of the teacher, effectiveness of the Bible study, acceptance of the class members, the opportunity for new members to exercise leadership in the class, and the ministry of the class all affect the ability to assimilate new members into the group.

The attitude of the teacher must be positive and enthusiastic to assimilate new members. If the teacher's attitude conveys apathy towards potential or new members, this attitude hinders the opportunity of the class to assimilate evangelistic prospects, potential new members, and new members. The teacher must be willing to outwardly show their love and concern for each and every person in the class. Since the teacher can effectively deal with only a small number of relationships at one time, the size of the class/Bible study group must be kept small enough for the teacher to develop and consistently encourage friendship with and among the members. Nothing creates apathy in teachers more than the feeling of being overwhelmed by the number of persons that already need the teacher's ministry which he or she cannot provide because the class is too large. The Sunday School class must remain small enough for the teacher to be able to adequately contact and encourage every member on a consistent basis.

The effectiveness of the Bible study also affects the ability of the class and church to assimilate new members. It has been said that bad teaching can empty classrooms faster than committed members can fill them. There is little doubt that members will not be present if the teaching is poorly prepared and not applicable to the needs of the members. Adequate preparation and planning are essential to consistently effective Bible study. It is amazing how few churches provide an efficient weekly planning time for its Sunday School leadership. Those same churches would think it appalling if the congregation would call a minister of music, and the minister of music said to the choir: "We really don't need to have choir rehearsal each week; just show up on Sunday morning and we'll all get together and sing." If it takes most choirs one-and-a-half to two hours to prepare to sing one anthem on Sunday morning, then what makes us think that the Sunday School leadership of the church does not need to meet for administration of the Sunday School, planning for Bible study, evangelism, assimilation of new members, and prayer? Unless training and support is given to teachers in a consistent and efficient manner there is a strong possibility that teaching will be weak and hinder the ability of the Sunday School to incorporate new members.

Not only is the attitude of the teacher important in the ability of the class to assimilate new members, but the attitude of the members is equally important. If the members of the class are not open and accepting of potential and new members, assimilation cannot occur. So much of human nature is involved here that one can honestly say that people will never be assimilated when the existing membership excludes potential and new members. The pastor may be wonderful, the Sunday School teacher may be great, but unless the members are open and accepting there will be little or no assimilation occurring in the life of the Sunday School and church.

Friendship is something that does not come naturally for some people. Two good books that can be used by Sunday School leadership to help members learn how to develop friendships within the church are: *The Friendship Factor*[2] and *Richer Relationships*.[3] The pastor and teachers of the church must continually encourage and teach members how to accept, love, and minister to potential and new members for assimilation to occur.

Potential and new members must also feel that there is opportunity for them to exercise leadership in the class if friendship and assimilation are to occur. This means that the class must make a conscious decision to allow potential and new members to be involved in leadership of the group. There are maintenance activities which are essential to the ability of any group to continue as a group. There must be encouragement, love, support, teaching materials, resources, fellowship activities, and so forth, in order for the group to continue as a group. It is possible to involve even potential members and certainly new members in these maintenance activities. For example, a potential new member might be asked to write an outline of the lesson on the chalkboard for the teacher. Or someone might be asked to make sure the chairs are arranged adequately for the teaching period. There is no reason why potential new members cannot be given a responsibility for these and many other kinds of activities in the class. Openness to involving potential and new members quickly in the leadership of the class helps to ensure quicker assimilation into the group. There are some activities and leadership positions that need to be reserved for more seasoned members but do not allow the existing membership to exclude potential and new members from assuming leadership responsibility for long periods of time, or you will begin to experience an assimilation problem.

When potential and new members come to Sunday School, they do not drop off their problems outside the door when they come to class. They come with all kinds of ministry needs. If these needs are not ministered to effectively and consistently, an assimilation problem will develop very quickly and may remain a problem for a long period of time and perhaps forever.

If you have at least one chronic absentee in your Sunday School, you have an assimilation problem. Have you ever wondered how people become chronic absentees? I can't imagine any Sunday School member consciously sitting down one day and saying, "My goal beginning right now is to become a chronic absentee in my Sunday School class." So how do they become chronic absentees? Perhaps it occurs something like this. One Sunday morning they get up and do not feel well. They decide to stay home and intend to attend Sunday School next Sunday. During the week no one from the Sunday School calls them or makes contact with them to see where they were or if there is a problem. The next Sunday they unexpectedly have company come into town, and their friends do not want to attend Sunday School and church. They stay home. During the week no one from the Sunday School calls them or makes contact with them to see where they were or if there is a problem. The next Sunday is the beginning of their two-weeks vacation. They go on vacation for two weeks, and when they arrive back home, no one from the Sunday School calls them or makes contact with them. There is not even a contact card in the mailbox when they get home from vacation. The next week they oversleep. Again they are not contacted, and by now they are out of the habit of attending, and they fear if they do go back they might be put on the spot in front of the whole class as to where they have been. Chronic absentees and assimilation problems begin because adequate ministry is not provided by the class or the Sunday School. The only way for the chronic absentee, assimilation, and ministry problems to be solved is by making sure that every potential member, new member, and long-time member of the Sunday School is contacted every week whether they attend or do not attend. It is only through this means that adequate and consistent ministry can be provided through the Sunday School.

If ineffective ministry is being provided through the Sunday School, there is already an assimilation problem in the Sunday School. This problem will just be compounded more and more as new members join the group but are not assimilated into the body.

**Small Group**

A Sunday School and church must have an adequate number of small groups for potential and new members to be a part of if it is to assimilate and conserve its evangelistic results. There should be at least seven groups for every 100 members of your church.[4] This averages out to be about 14-15 people per group. Interestingly, this is about the suggested size of an adult Sunday School class. The larger the church, the more small groups are needed in order to effectively assimilate and conserve the results of evangelism and church growth. This small-group factor must be kept in mind as a church continues to grow. If a church is averaging 12-15 new members each Sunday, it is in essence adding a new Sunday School class every Sunday. If new Sunday School classes and other small groups are not organized to incorporate these new people as they join, it will be very difficult for these persons to become assimilated into the church.

## Lay Leadership

The ability of any church to assimilate new members largely depends upon the quality and openness of the lay leadership of the church. Lay leaders of the church must be taught barriers to assimilation and helped to gain insight into how to overcome these barriers. As the lay leaders are equipped to deal with both the emotional and practical barriers to the church's growth, the church is more fully equipped to incorporate potential and new members into the life of the church.

On every committee and in every group there ought to be approximately 20 percent of the committee or group who have joined the church in the past two years.[5] Many churches have a difficult time accepting this important fact and, therefore, do not do an effective job of assimilating potential and new members and, therefore, do not grow significantly or at all.

## Time

Time is of the utmost importance when it comes to effectively assimilating new members and conserving the results of evangelism. The longer that a person goes without developing friendships, becoming involved in a leadership position, taking part in small-group activities, and feeling accepted into the body life of the church, the more likely the person will not become assimilated into the body.

The first six weeks are absolutely critical in the assimilation process. Unless new members and those recently reached for Christ have found a friend, become involved in the Sunday School, or are taking part in some type of church activity, the chance of them being incorporated is very slim. The church must develop a specific and systematic way to ensure that the assimilation process begins as soon as the person joins the church and continues until the person is adequately assimilated.

## Accountability

In order to conserve the results of evangelism and church growth, leaders and members in the church must be held accountable for making sure the assimilation process is functioning effectively. The Sunday School class becomes a crucial element of the process through its weekly contacting of individuals through the Sunday School. Every person who is a part of any organization has some level of responsibility in helping to conserve and assimilate the results of evangelism. These leaders must be held accountable for follow-up and ministry to new members.

## Homogeneity

Assimilation often depends upon a factor we call the homogeneous principle, the observation that most people and churches feel more comfortable with and thus attract people who are most similar to themselves. What this means is that the more homogeneous the group, the more difficult it is to attract people who are different than those who are members of that group. This has several implications which help the process of assimilation but can also hinder the process of assimilation.

Awareness of the homogeneous principle is often helpful in the assimilation process because you can make some fairly accurate assumptions about what you need to do to attract the people who are most like the existing group. For example, if your church is made up primarily of young urban professionals, you will probably not have too great a difficulty reaching other young urban professionals. You can assume some things about what it will take to attract young urban professionals and what it will take to assimilate and keep them in the church. This principle provides great advantages in the planning and allocating of resources, programs, and so forth, in order to reach and assimilate people into the body of Christ.

There is a danger with this principle, however. If we begin to use the homogeneous principle and fail to set priorities for reaching people who are different than the homogeneous group to which we belong, we not only hinder our ability to assimilate new members and conserve our evangelistic results, but we also fail to follow the biblical teachings to share the gospel with every kind of person, not just people like ourselves.

There are many programs that we can develop to help ensure that we are adequately concerned about conserving and assimilating the results of our evangelistic outreach and witness. New Member Training and the ways in which we hold new members accountable for their membership and growth is just one area where we can make a positive impact on our ability to retain the results of our evangelistic efforts. One such program for new members is the Barnabas Program.

## The Barnabas Program

The Barnabas Program is based on the life of Barnabas—an encourager of new converts in the faith. In Acts 4:36 Luke told us, "Joseph, a Levite from Cyprus, whom the apostles called Barnabas (which means Son of Encouragement), sold a field he owned and brought the money and put it at the apostles feet" (NIV). This tells us that encouragement was a life-style for Barnabas. In other places in the New Testament we gain insight into the power of encouragement through the life of Barnabas. It was Barnabas who, when the apostles feared Paul after his Damascus road experience, recommended that Paul be accepted by the apostolic group (Gal. 2:1-10). It was also Barnabas who provided encouragement to John Mark after the first missionary journey. When Paul was unwilling to take John Mark along on the second trip, Barnabas took John Mark with him. Through this, John Mark gained the experience needed to become a more mature disciple and was encouraged to eventually write the Gospel of Mark. If New Testament scholars are correct concerning the dating of the Gospel of Mark and the Synoptic view of Mark, Matthew, and

Luke, then Barnabas through his encouragement affected three of the Gospels through his encouragement of John Mark and almost two thirds of the New Testament through his encouragement of Paul.

The Barnabas Program consists of eight distinct elements including the purpose, the method, enlistment, training, assignment, follow-up, and encourager responsibilities.

### Purpose

As men and women, boys and girls, come to know Jesus Christ as Savior and Lord through the efforts of the Sunday School's outreach and evangelism, the desire is to see them become grounded in the Bible and the family of faith. When persons accept Christ, there are many changes that come about in their lives and numerous questions to be answered. Second Corinthians 5:17 says: "If any man be in Christ, he is a new creature: old things are passed away; behold, all things are become new" (KJV). There is a radical change in the new Christian's life as the old things are passed away, and all things become new. According to Matthew 28:20 it is our responsibility to help each individual mature in the faith by becoming active in Sunday School, worship, and evangelism.

The *Survival Kit*, written by Ralph W. Neighbor, Jr., is an excellent guide for new Christians as they grow in their knowledge of the Bible, Christ, the church, and their relationships to each of these.[6] The *Survival Kit* is a great book, but unless it is studied and completed it will contribute little to the new Christian's spiritual life. The Barnabas Program is a plan to help the new member get established in the Bible through the use of the *Survival Kit* and to provide an encourager to assist him or her in getting involved in all aspects of church life and finishing the *Survival Kit*.

### Method

The Sunday School is the best organization to administer the Barnabas Program for three reasons:

(1) Bible study is the central program of the New Testament church to disciple Christians.

(2) The organization is already there to administer the program.

(3) Using the Sunday School will make it easy for an encourager to make contact with their survivor.

Implementation of the Barnabas Program through the Sunday School will immediately relate the new Christians to a person in their Bible study department/class. As someone they see every Sunday in Sunday School helps them, they will catch some of the things that are hard to teach. They will get a lot of answers by what they see in others' lives. We can see many desirable results by using this method:

- Faithful attendance in Sunday School
- Faithful attendance in worship services
- Faithful attendance at training events
- Attendance at visitation
- Involvement in department fellowships

### Enlistment

The heart of the program is the enlistment of encouragers. Without an ample supply of encouragers the program will fail. It is important to make known the need, the purpose, and the program. Enlistment of encouragers can best be done in the Sunday School class department period. Utilize the department outreach/evangelism leader. This person can explain the program to your people and enlist those who are interested.

The church newsletter and the pastor's endorsement will help in the enlistment process. The enlistment process will work best if each person enlisted is asked to sign a commitment card. As God blesses the faithfulness of His people, He will send more and more people to be a part of the church family.

The most effective place for this process to take place is through the Sunday School. The Sunday School can be a place where people can study God's Word and come to Jesus Christ as their personal Lord and Savior. If it is to fulfill this purpose, then we must plan for it to happen. There are millions of people who need to experience Jesus Christ. The Sunday School is the greatest organization ever invented to get people in touch with Christ. Therefore, let us fulfill the Great Commission and evangelize our world quickly, and let us do it through the Sunday School.

## Notes

1. R. Wayne Jones, *Using Spiritual Gifts* (Nashville: Broadman Press, 1985).

2. Alan McGinnis, *The Friendship Factor* (Minneapolis: Augsburg Press, 1979).

3. Myron Rush, *Richer Relationships* (Wheaton: Victor Books, 1983)

4. C. Peter Wagner, *Church Growth State of the Art* (Wheaton: Tyndale House, 1988) 97.

5. Ibid., 100.

6. Ralph W. Neighbor, Jr., *Survival Kit for New Christians* (Nashville: Convention Press, 1979).

## Training

Training of encouragers may be accomplished in a two-session seminar. During these two sessions the following areas will be covered:

- Why through the Sunday School?
- Who gets a *Survival Kit?*
- What is in the *Survival Kit?*
- What does an encourager do?
- How does the program work?

## Assignment

Assignment of encouragers to new members are made the first of the week immediately after a person has been baptized. The assignments are men to men and women to women within the Sunday School Department to the extent that this is possible.

## Follow-Up

The encouragers themselves are encouraged periodically by a contact from the church office.

## Encourager Responsibilities

- Deliver the Kit
- Make regular contact until the Kit is completed
- Be an example

Whatever program is used to help you assimilate and conserve the results of evangelism in your Sunday School and church, it must be consistent and effective. If it is not, there will always be a vital part of the evangelization process that is left to be accomplished. We cannot say that we have truly evangelized until we have also congregationalized. Conserving and assimilating the results of evangelism is a first step in this process. It is the key to not only sustained church growth but continued spiritual growth in the life of every individual we evangelize.

## Training

Training of encouragers may be accomplished in a two-session seminar. During these two sessions the following areas will be covered:

- Why through the Sunday School?
- Who gets a *Survival Kit?*
- What is in the *Survival Kit?*
- What does an encourager do?
- How does the program work?

## Assignment

Assignment of encouragers to new members are made the first of the week immediately after a person has been baptized. The assignments are men to men and women to women within the Sunday School Department to the extent that this is possible.

## Follow-Up

The encouragers themselves are encouraged periodically by a contact from the church office.

## Encourager Responsibilities

- Deliver the Kit
- Make regular contact until the Kit is completed
- Be an example

Whatever program is used to help you assimilate and conserve the results of evangelism in your Sunday School and church, it must be consistent and effective. If it is not, there will always be a vital part of the evangelization process that is left to be accomplished. We cannot say that we have truly evangelized until we have also congregationalized. Conserving and assimilating the results of evangelism is a first step in this process. It is the key to not only sustained church growth but continued spiritual growth in the life of every individual we evangelize.

The most effective place for this process to take place is through the Sunday School. The Sunday School can be a place where people can study God's Word and come to Jesus Christ as their personal Lord and Savior. If it is to fulfill this purpose, then we must plan for it to happen. There are millions of people who need to experience Jesus Christ. The Sunday School is the greatest organization ever invented to get people in touch with Christ. Therefore, let us fulfill the Great Commission and evangelize our world quickly, and let us do it through the Sunday School.

## Notes

1. R. Wayne Jones, *Using Spiritual Gifts* (Nashville: Broadman Press, 1985).

2. Alan McGinnis, *The Friendship Factor* (Minneapolis: Augsburg Press, 1979).

3. Myron Rush, *Richer Relationships* (Wheaton: Victor Books, 1983).

4. C. Peter Wagner, *Church Growth State of the Art* (Wheaton: Tyndale House, 1988) 97.

5. Ibid., 100.

6. Ralph W. Neighbor, Jr., *Survival Kit for New Christians* (Nashville: Convention Press, 1979).